WILLIAM BUCKLAND

1734-1774

Architect of
Virginia and Maryland

by

ROSAMOND RANDALL ⌊BEIRNE

and

JOHN HENRY SCARFF, F.A.I.A.

Baltimore · THE MARYLAND HISTORICAL SOCIETY · 1958

WILLIAM BUCKLAND

Portrait by Charles Willson Peale,
begun 1774, completed 1787.
Imaginative symbolic background displays
the base of a monumental column and an
uncommon five column portico.

*Dedicated to Those
Who in the 17th and 18th Centuries
Planted in America the Seeds
of English Culture*

Preface

So LITTLE is known about any of our colonial architects that it seems not too presumptuous to attempt to frame this unfinished sketch of a man who deserves recognition.

The urge to develop the biography of William Buckland was an inherited one. It was stimulated by the study of a few family papers and a close association of one of the authors for many years with Buckland's Annapolis houses. Every family has its traditions but most lack a member with time and energy to put these traditions in some sort of permanent form. A professional knowledge of the byways and ancient mores of London and Oxford, as well as of the finer points of eighteenth century architecture, was needed to round out the story of Buckland's career. Therefore, the two authors became associated in an effort to recreate the life of one of the few pre-Revolutionary craftsmen whose buildings still stand today, serene and authenticated. His is typical of the traditional American success story—the poor young man's progress and rise in the world. Though his opportunities lay more in the domestic field than in public works, they are unrivaled in his time and place.

We have many acknowledgments to make, some of which fall more naturally into the notes. Chiefly are the authors grateful to the late Daniel R. Randall for his pioneering in William Buckland's cause. To encouraging friends, particularly to Francis C. Haber, who patiently read and condensed the manuscript, and to Edith Rossiter Bevan; to the courteous staffs of the British Museum, The Public Record Office, the libraries of the Guildhall and of the Royal Institute of British Architects, the manuscript room of the Bodleian Library, the Manuscript Division of the Library of Congress, the Peabody Institute, the Maryland Historical Society, the late Roger Thomas of the Maryland Hall of Records, the Virginia State Library, the Virginia Historical Society, the library of the College of William and Mary, and the Alderman Library of the University of Virginia, we offer our sincere thanks.

R. R. B.
J. H. S.

Contents

List of Illustrations

xi

WILLIAM BUCKLAND
1734-1774

Architect of
Virginia and Maryland

I

English Background

Sixteen miles west-northwest of Oxford, on the Windrush River, a tributary of the Thames, is the town of Burford. Its name signifies a ford by a hill. Burford has figured in English history since Saxon times and is known today for its wool industries and its quarries of excellent building stone. In this ancient town the parish register records that on May 30, 1733, Francis Buckland and Mary Dunsdown, "both of this parish," were married by licence. Normally an English marriage took place after banns were announced in church, but without banns marriage could be lawfully celebrated by virtue of licence issued by the bishop or archdeacon, or by his surrogate. Soon thereafter Francis and Mary Buckland must have moved, for the parish register of St. Peter's-in-the-East at Oxford records that "William, son of Francis Buckland" was baptized. Later by William's own hand we learn that he was "born in the Parish of St. Peter's-in-the-East in the City of Oxford on the 14th day of Augt 1734."[1] It was this William who was to leave his native land, cross the Atlantic and join the colonists of Virginia and Maryland, and be intrusted by several of the most influential among them with the design of their fine residences.

Francis Buckland called himself a yeoman, indicating that he was or had been an independent freeholder. At the time of his marriage England was undergoing economic and agricultural changes which increased the mobility of the population and affected the status of the farming classes. In the regions adjacent to London the demand for market produce stimulated the movement of enclosure of commons and the expansion of tillable land. Many freeholders sold their ancient rights and lands and with the cash took up lands or leaseholds elsewhere. Others were drawn to manufacturing centers, either to work as

1

laborers or to find lands closer to good markets. When Francis Buckland moved from Burford to Oxford between May 30, 1733, and August 14, 1734, he may have sold his inherited lands and taken up a long term leasehold or purchased lands which would be near the market at Oxford. In any event, the title of yeoman placed him in a station of some dignity in English society at this time. The yeoman commanded respect among the hired laborers and on occasion he mingled with the squirearchy.

The life of the Buckland family centered in St. Peter's-in-the-East where its baptisms, marriages and burials are recorded. St. Peter's-in-the-East is situated on Queen's Lane (formerly St. Edmund's Hall Lane) as it passes the buildings of New College. Parts of the church date from Norman times and its crypt is of the late Middle Ages. A small amount of seventeenth century glass remains. Parts of the tower are fourteenth century work although the parapet and quatrefoils are later. On the walls one can read memorial tablets to the more important parishioners of other days.

The graveyard lies on three sides of the church between the College and St. Edmund's Hall. The grave stones crowd close in and all except the most recent are illegible. In the course of centuries, adjacent buildings have encroached upon church property and many graves have been obliterated. Salvaged headstones, upon which not a vestige remains of the inscriptions are ranged against the enclosing wall, and under the overhanging trees of the College gardens they gather moss. There unmarked, forgotten Bucklands lie buried and their dust has mingled with the soil of their native land.

In the faded and dusty records in the parish chests it is impossible now to ascertain relationships, for between 1734 when William was baptized and 1780 when a Francis was buried, there are many references to "Francis." In 1736 "Francis, son of Francis Buckland" was baptized and two years later "John, son of Francis Buckland." They would appear to be younger brothers of William. Unfortunately, during those years the mother's name is not mentioned in baptisms, so we cannot be sure. Later there is an entry: "Buried Jan. 3, 1739 Mary Buckland." That must be the Mary who married Francis Buckland in Burford just six years before! It was but a year after John was born.

The frequently recurring name "Francis" is to be a puzzle to the end. It is recorded that in 1746 and again in 1747 children of a "Francis Buckland" were baptized without reference to the mother. In 1749 a "Thomas, son of Francis and Penelope Buckland," was baptized. Was Thomas the brother of the children born in 1746 and 1747, and had Francis, the father of William, married the second time? It is not known. After 1749 there is a lapse of eleven years without entries relating to Bucklands. Then in 1758 another Francis, son of "Francis and Mary Buckland," is baptized. This father could well be the Francis who was born in 1736, and the brother of our William in America, for he would have been twenty-two years of age.

There were undoubtedly several families named Buckland in the parish, since Buckland entries appear frequently until 1790, when they cease, and the name still exists in Oxfordshire. There is no apparent connection between the families of William Buckland the architect and William Buckland (1784-1856), Dean of Westminster, scholar and teacher at the University of Oxford, and leading geologist of England in the 1820's. Dean Buckland was born in Axminster, eldest son of the rector of Templeton and Trusham in Devon. Curiously, however, Dean William Buckland named his son Francis.

The family at St. Peter's-in-the-East pursued its humble course and took but a small and unnoticed part in the large drama of its time. If it had not been for one among them who at the age of fourteen decided to turn his back upon the ways of his fathers to seek his fortune in the more promising life of London, history would be without mention of them. They would have played their parts in the splendid sweep of the eighteenth century unknown and unrecorded. The not inconsiderable talents of William, son of Francis, yeoman, set him apart and entitle him to some renown among the creative men of colonial America.

Throughout the eighteenth century Oxfordshire remained a country of agriculture and pasturage. In its various districts the soil, the vegetation and the architecture present local characteristics directly traceable to the rock that underlies them. Burford, where Francis and Mary Buckland lived before they were married in 1733, is a neighborhood of important quarries. From them came stone for the rebuilding of the Oxford colleges and by clumsy barges it was shipped down the river Thames as far as London for the building of St. Paul's Cathedral after the Great Fire of 1666. From the forests of the county timber was supplied for the building of houses and ships. Another great resource of Oxfordshire is clay good for the making of bricks. The county up to modern times has not attained any great industrial importance, though the Thames and its tributaries made traffic with London easy before the advent of good road transportation. During his formative years William Buckland in Oxford must have heard much talk of building and it seems most natural for the talented boy to have had his attention so directed and later to have his ambition turned towards the metropolis where his father's brother, James, a joiner, lived.

William Buckland Son of ffrauris Buckland of the City of Oxford yeoman puts to James Buckand Citizen and Jomer of London for seven years by Indentures Dated this day

Cous: $10 Charity from the University school of Oxford —

APPRENTICE RECORD

Thus comes an important date in the life of William Buckland. In 1748, when he had reached the age of fourteen years, he was apprenticed to his uncle James, " a citizen and Joiner of London." [2] How did it happen that the eldest son of yeoman Francis chose to learn a craft? One can only surmise. That he had a decided talent is certain. If his father had taken a leasehold, his patrimony, as eldest son, was uncertain. This would have made the opportunities for a skilled laborer unpromising. The Oxford colleges were being rebuilt in the new style and he would be quite familiar with the more interesting and rewarding life of the skilled craftsman, but Oxford was a small market-town where life offered him few diversions or opportunities. Life in Londontown promised adventure and advancement. Many country boys, before and since, have been in William's position and chosen as he did. His mother had been dead for nine years. This hardship, and the reputable character of his yeoman background may have been the cause of his being given financial assistance by one of the charitable organizations of Oxford to pursue a craft.

London in the year 1748, when Buckland began his apprenticeship as joiner, had about three-quarters of a million inhabitants. It extended from the great royal palace on the west, from Oxford Street on the north, along the river to Tower Hill. South of the river, between Westminster Bridge and London Bridge, was Southwark with Lambeth Palace opposite Wapping. The name London extended over two cities, one borough and about forty-six ancient villages, one of which was Holborn where James Buckland, the joiner, lived.

The old wall was being gradually removed and all around were market gardens tended by women. Nearly the whole city had been rebuilt after the Great Fire. It had lost its picturesque gables, pent houses, casement windows and ancient churches. The rebuilt houses were in line. Windows were high and provided with sliding sash. The highways only were paved with stones and there were no gutters. Posts for the protection of pedestrians were located at short intervals along sidewalks without curbs. Water ran down the middle of the street, making frequent puddles. Carts and wagons splashed the passerby. Peddlers called their wares. Sign boards swinging noisily from almost every house added to the uproar of the streets. Nuisances against which the townsmen had to contend were ordure, especially at the posterns of the city, rubbish in heaps, broken pavements, ruinous houses, sheds and stalls blocking streets, encroachment of newly built houses, bullocks being driven through the streets, mad dogs, swarms of beggars, and an absence of lighting. Every householder was required at night to hang out a lantern from six to eleven. By eleven the streets were in total darkness and those unfortunates obliged to go out were accompanied by link boys carrying torches.

Water was supplied by springs, wells and pumps and not till mid-century did all streets have water pipes. In 1736 citizens complained that robbers increased daily in numbers and in audacity. The question of lighting streets was then considered. The numbering of houses commenced and signs obstructing the streets were removed or put back against the walls.

Speculators in land were laying out the London squares. Grey's Inn, between the Temple and Holborn, was among the first. Montagu House, which a few years later was to be taken for the site of the British Museum, marked the limit of the city to the north. Beyond it lay fields or ruins of old monastic houses, but the metropolitan area was reaching out into the agricultural surroundings and new and more talent was in great demand for the public building enterprises which were replacing the old palaces and filling the needs of a rapidly expanding population.

To this great magnet William Buckland was attracted in the spring of 1748. His uncle James was a citizen and householder living on Dean Street in Holborn and a member of the Joiners Company. Four years earlier, in 1744, James Buckland had taken his nephew Thomas, son of his brother John, " of the City of Oxford, Yeoman," as an apprentice but he still needed help.[3] A second nephew would be a welcome addition to the family on Dean street for James had no son of his own. Although the shop took the entire street floor there was room above for the family and the two boys could occupy a room on the top floor.

For the next seven years, as William grew from boyhood to man's estate, he lost his country ways and shy manners. Living in his uncle's family he could apply himself to mastering his chosen craft. He had every opportunity to observe the building all about him and to study what books he could borrow. From his later work it is easy to see that from the specialized activities of the joiner's trade his attention was directed towards the broader field of the master-builder.

James Buckland is listed in the records of " The Worshipful Company of Joiners " as a " Journeyman " paying three pence the quarter during 1743-44, and as a " householder " paying six pence the quarter from 1744 to 1749. His address is given as Dean Street, Holborn, a street known today as Dane Street.[4] It is one block long extending halfway between High Holborn and Red Lion Square. It is shown on Rocque's map of London published in 1746. But two houses exist that might be remainders of the days of James Buckland. These are three and four stories high, of brick without any architectural embellishments.

The guild of the Worshipful Company of Joiners had been in existence since 1309 and, after the Great Fire, built its hall on Freyer Lane on Dowgate Hill near one of the four original gates of the city. The guilds were originally voluntary associations formed for religious, social, charitable or funerary purposes. There were, also, purely religious guilds composed mainly of the clergy, social religious guilds for the performance of religious exercises, trade guilds, merchant and craft, or artist guilds. From such associations grew the City Companies, of which the Worshipful Company of Joiners was one. These were primarily for the purpose of protecting the consumer and employer from incompetency and fraud but also for the protection of the skilled worker. New members were formally admitted and had to swear to obey and preserve the secrets of the trade. Each company had its master, its wardens, assistants and apprentices, and its livery. The companies served as benefit societies by which the workman and his family, in return for contributions, were protected in ill health and old age. They also built almshouses and schools, established charitable foundations, and had something of the character of modern clubs, for feasting and social intercourse were regular features.

The London Companies constituted a body politic, sharing in the rule of the city. They nominated the Mayor and at one time the members of Parliament from the city. Originally their chief object was the promotion of the prosperity of the trade with which they were associated and by charter to " settle and govern their mysteries." Unlike the labor unions of today, membership was composed of both employer and employee and was obtained by patrimony, apprenticeship, or payment of a fee. In the eighteenth century there were twelve " great companies " and sixty-two minor ones.

The Joiners' Company was one of the specialized craft guilds which had grown out of the medieval Carpenter's Company. The joiner was the workman who joined pieces of wood with glue or nails or by means of grooves, dovetails and framing. He, therefore, was the maker of furniture, the framed wainscotting which replaced the plain boarded walls of medieval times, and the mantelpiece and door frame. But if the work was to be enriched with much ornamentation, the joiner called in the ceiler who was not a plasterer but a woodworker. To " ceil " was to cover the bare walls and ceiling rafters with ornamental woodwork.

Timber framed houses were going out of fashion long before the Great Fire made them, as far as London was concerned, illegal. There was a tendency to lessen and simplify the work of the carpenter. Fixed furniture could be made by carpenters but from all forms of carving he was debarred. He was limited to plain construction and had but a small part in the woodwork of a period remarkable for the abundance and excellence of the joiners' work.

The right of entry into the trade was jealously guarded and could only be through the strait and narrow gate of apprenticeship. The aspirant was required to produce some elaborate and costly evidence of his skill—the proof-piece or "master-piece." This requirement had become general in London by the seventeenth century. The ordinary journeyman could afford neither the money nor time and many refused to make the master-piece which they claimed was an unlawful restraint on the entry into the trade. But the Joiners' Company claimed that the practice was without controversy or refusal within the city. There seems no doubt that the master-piece was used as a barrier against the flood of journeymen that masters wished to keep in the position of wage earners.

The usual term of apprenticeship was seven years but " not less than four." Terms were covered by an indenture, or " indented " contract, in which were carefully set out the duties and obligations of each party. The paper on which the terms were stated was cut into two parts by a zig-zag or " indented " line which later could be fitted together, thus proving the authenticity of each part. The laws covering the relationship of master and apprentice were fully codified.[5]

Each party to an apprenticeship indenture undertook to do certain things. The apprentice promised to " faithfully serve, his secrets keep, his lawful commandments everywhere gladly do. He will not contract matrimony [this was later declared illegal], nor play cards or dice. He will neither buy nor sell, nor haunt taverns." The master, in consideration of a premium, promised to teach and instruct as best he could, and to provide meat, drink, apparel, washing and lodging, in sickness and in health.

There was considerable difference between apprenticeship and hiring. " An apprentice is a person who by contract is to be taught a trade, in contradistinction from a person who engages to serve generally." When the contract was executed with the solemnities incident to a binding by deed, and the agreement was to instruct the party serving, it was considered a contract of apprenticeship. Instruments of apprenticeship had to be stamped by crown officials at the master's expense and the consideration fully set out. Indentures were dissolved by the apprentice coming of age, by the bankruptcy of the master, or by consent. In some of the American colonies the assignment of indentures of apprenticeship was authorized by statute.

The apprentice was entitled to wages (except when he might be imprisoned), but the master was entitled to all his earnings. The master also had more authority over him than over a servant, for he could legally " correct " the boy for negligence or other misbehavior provided it was done with moderation. Any unnecessary violence or degradation was illegal. An apprentice could be dismissed only when the indenture gave in express terms the power to do so. The master was entitled to the custody of the indenture until the end of the term when it must be given up to the apprentice, certifying that the apprenticeship had been properly served. Before the establishment of technical schools the system was an effective means of teaching the various trades.

Under such conditions William Buckland, on the fifth day of April, 1748, was indentured for seven years by his father, Francis, to his uncle James, citizen and joiner of London. " Consideration to the master: £10 Charity from the University School of Oxford "—probably a foundation of which there were many for the education of boys in the trades and crafts—was mentioned in the agreement.[6]

Young Buckland commenced his apprenticeship at an auspicious time for the mastery of the building art. The new style of architecture introduced into England by Inigo Jones upon his return from Italy in 1619 where he had been profoundly influenced by the work of Palladio had been adapted to English taste by Christopher Wren and others. Gothic architecture had gone out of vogue and country houses, as well as public buildings, were brought under the classical " Palladian " style.

Probably at no time in the history of English architecture has there existed a more perfect knowledge of the technical arts of building than during the first part of the eighteenth century. There was available a trained and highly intelligent school of masons, carpenters and joiners, often men of talent and understanding of the arts and crafts. In the paneling, the delicate adjustment of detail to window and cornice, cupboard and mantelpiece, there is refinement and precision of workmanship. It would be hard to find a more habitable dwelling than the plain red brick house with its white cornice and sash windows that became during the Georgian period the home of the ordinary Englishman both in England and in the colonies of North America. The effectiveness of Georgian architecture owes much to the excellent craftsmanship of the period. The best of the English builders absorbed all that they had learned from other countries and through their own intelligence adapted it to the traditions and needs of their own nation. The ability to assimilate and express their own traditions is a measure of their capacity. It is that which gives to their work the quality of style and lasting value.

The apprenticeship gave to Buckland a mastery of the craftsmanship of the period, while all around him excellent models of the new style of architecture were educating his taste. There was also a continuous stream of good books on architecture flowing from the press: Colin Campbell's *Vitruvius Britannicus* (London, 1715), Giacomo Leoni's *Architecture of A. Palladio* (London, 1715), James Gibbs' *Book of Architecture* (London, 1728), the designs of Inigo Jones published by Isaac Ware in 1735, and others. It is interesting to note that many of the significant architectural works of the period were listed in the inventory of William Buckland made at the time of his death (see Appendix E).

Buckland's seven-year apprenticeship to his uncle would have ended in April, 1755, when by custom he was entitled to the " Freedom of the Company," as becoming a member of the Joiners' guild was called. Proof of ability and payment of a fee were required. Fifty-six apprentices were admitted to the freedom of the company that year but the name of William Buckland is not among them.[7] His uncle James is credited on the books of the Joiners' Company with payment of his quarterage dues during 1749 but with nothing beyond that date. He might have died or he might simply have ceased payments. Without his uncle as sponsor it may have been impossible for William to become a member of the company, or he may have decided that there was no need to pay the fee since he had a job signed and sealed, and that in a land far away.

About this time Thomson Mason, the younger son of a relatively wealthy and prominent Virginia family, who had been studying law as a member of the Middle Temple, was ready to return home when he received a letter from his brother George asking him to find a well trained and reliable man to provide the interior for his new house. Thomson, who was completely dependent on his brother, even for pocket money, set about looking for the right man, as the smallest favor he could do in return for the best of educations. George had inherited through primogeniture his father's entire estate but too late to avail himself of an English education. His feeling of responsibility for his brother was matched only by that for his wife and growing family, for whom he wished to build a comfortable and elegant house. Having had William Buckland well recommended to him, Thomson Mason immediately engaged him by a four-year indenture.[8] This was the very best contract a penniless young man could make. The cost of a berth and decent food on a ship going to the colonies was about twenty pounds and the uncertainty of employment there worked hardships on all those who did not have a reserve to fall back upon. So on the fourth of August, 1755, Buckland signed the contract to serve Thomson Mason, " his executors or assigns in the Plantations of Virginia, Beyond the seas for the space of four years as a Carpenter and Joiner." Thomson Mason agreed to pay his passage and keep. " To provide for and allow the said William Buckland all necessary meat, drink, washing, lodging fit and convenient for him as covenant Servants in such cases . . . and pay . . . the said William Buckland wages or salary at the rate of twenty pounds sterling per annum, payable quarterly." [9] This was good pay for an inexperienced though well-trained man, as it is a matter of record that schoolmasters received as little as five pounds per annum. Proof that Buckland was penniless is shown by the record written on the back of the indenture of two loans of cash from Mason. On the 4th of August he borrowed against his future salary one pound seven shillings and on the following day he received three pounds thirteen shillings, making five pounds in all. This sum was undoubtedly needed to purchase an outfit before he left behind him the well-stocked London shops.

Turning his face away from the Oxford of his boyhood and the London of his apprenticeship, William Buckland cast his lot with a new acquaintance and the colonies beyond the seas.

Arms of the Worshipful
Company of Joiners

II

Virginia and the Masons

THE TWO young men, Mason and Buckland, both
turning twenty-one, both inexperienced but enthusiastic over their
chosen professions, presumably set sail on the same ship on the 5th of
August.[1] In the close confinement of a long voyage in a small vessel the
formalities of the British social system were generally forgotten. The
accommodations differed little except where indentured servants were
transported as a money-making cargo. Buckland would have had a
berth and " officer's food " and the opportunity to be on fairly intimate
terms with his employer. The average length of the voyage, because
of prevailing head winds, was eight weeks to the Virginia Capes. Sometimes as much as two weeks was eliminated on the return trip to
England but storms, unpredictable then as now, caused havoc to any
schedule. The largest of the Virginia ports was Yorktown where the
masts of one hundred ocean-going ships could often be seen. If the
vessel bearing Mason and Buckland ended its journey there, two
choices awaited the travelers. They could have transferred to a Potomac
River packet which made stops at Colchester, Alexandria, and even at
George Mason's own landing in Occoquan Creek, or they could have
hired horses and taken the highway inland to Chappawamsic, Stafford County, where Mason's mother lived. Due to the uncertainty of
the mails between England and the colonies and the gamble of wind
and weather, the arrival of the travelers would have been unannounced
to a welcoming family.

If they missed a river craft, and were impatient to be on their way,
they would have hired horses at the nearest inn and left their traveling

boxes to be forwarded by boat. The Yorktown highway, a well supervised road, led west twelve miles to the capital city of Williamsburg.
Here was a pretty little town with comfortable houses set in gardens
along three or four tree-lined streets. There was nothing pretentious
about it except the Governor's Palace and the Capitol. Williamsburg
was purely the seat of government and without great importance in the
social or economic life of Virginia except when the Assembly was
meeting. The population did not grow normally. Because the only
newspaper in the colony was printed there and because of the ambitious
shops catering to the gentry, a certain businesslike bustle was periodi-
cally discernible on court days. It gave Buckland a sense of wellbeing
to see familiar signs over sidewalks advertising coachmakers, peruque
makers, cabinet makers, silversmiths and the like. He was not to live
in a wilderness after all!

Their ride of over one hundred miles could be accomplished in
three days in good weather, but it was seldom so done. There were
rivers to be crossed by ferry and hundreds of cattle gates blocking the
highway. These had to be opened and closed. There were also friends
of Thomson Mason's living too near their path to be passed by without
a word of greeting after a four year absence. A matter of four days was
always allowed to get the representatives from Fairfax and Stafford
counties to their elected position in Williamsburg.[2] This was travel
by " chariot " or " chair," as their various carriages were called. It can
be presumed that the riders would have taken an equal length of time
to reach their destination, Chappawamsic.

Summer had passed on the voyage over. Autumn in Virginia was
almost as breath-taking as spring. The prolific dogwoods and gum
trees brought an early red to the landscape. The varying shades of
yellow in poplar, maple and birch blended with the russets of great oaks
against a background of ever-present pines. A sharp early frost had
ripened the persimmons and dampened the deep summer dust of the
roads. It also blackened the last of the summer flowers, golden rod and
asters. There were vast stretches of virgin forest broken at intervals by
rutted roads leading into more tillable meadow land. Where fields were
under cultivation along the highway, the tobacco had long been cut,
leaving disorder in stubby stems and dropped leaves. Only the fodder
corn stood gaunt and shabby where it had grown.

Jogging along the sandy road, past one great plantation after another, Buckland could compare the long ragged distance between even a sight of a house or person with the neat English highways leading from town to town and inn to inn. Except for an occasional group of Negroes working in a field or mending fences, hours would pass without sight of a human being. It was hard to believe that Virginia contained one-fifth of all the inhabitants of the colonies.

Narrow roads, sometimes five miles long, led in to the great houses. These were the carriage entrances. Plantation owners often considered their water landing as their front entrance. Because of the innumerable estuaries of the James, York, Rappahannock and Potomac rivers, water travel was simple—simple at least for those who owned boats. Barges rowed by slaves took the great landowners to church and to near neighbors. Snows (square-rigged vessels), took their hogsheads of tobacco from the end of a " rolling road " to central warehouses or direct to agents in Liverpool, London or Glasgow. Schooners carried larger cargoes of tobacco and brought back from Britain goods for the merchants' stores, filling the diversified needs of the colonists.

About halfway between Aquia Church and the town of Dumfries, on the northern border of Stafford County, the travelers would have found the Mason home. Little is known of Chappawamsic except that the widowed Mrs. George Mason, senior, had chosen it as her dower right. The house was built of stone from nearby Aquia quarry and designed at an earlier and simpler period.[3] One can imagine with what joy the two young men reached the end of their journey, whether by land or by water; Mason to be home once more and William Buckland to begin his life's work.

The Virginia of 1755 may have been unlike the vision that William Buckland had of it when he signed his papers in London. It is most unlikely, however, that a Mason ever tried to deceive him, for honesty in thought and deed was with them a *sine qua non*. The colony was now one hundred and fifty years old with many third generation settlers who no longer spoke of Great Britain as " home " and who called the newcomers " Englishmen." It was a land of contrasts, not so much in the characteristics of its inhabitants as in the opportunities offered them to rise from a lower level to that of wealth and power.[4]

Great fortunes could no longer be made in land and tobacco in

Tidewater Virginia. The early settlers had already exhausted those sources of wealth. Land-speculation was still a business, however, as the western lands were opened. The early landed-gentry were a powerful class who voted themselves into offices and were hand in glove with his Majesty's official deputy, the Governor. This proud group was augmented by a few British-trained barristers, practicing at the county courts and twice a year at the General Court held in Williamsburg. Other well educated men were the clergy of the Established Church, all ordained in England, for no Bishop had ever been appointed for the colonies, in spite of an urgent need. Some of these parish incumbents were mere politicians looking for a living; some were trained in medicine and were highly valued in both capacities. The only other learned profession was teaching. Teachers were ill paid; could be bought as indentured servants fresh from the old country or tempted from halls of learning in the North. The College of William and Mary at Williamsburg was attended only by those enthusiasts for an education who could not afford the luxury of Oxford or Cambridge. Often the teaching profession was but a stepping-stone to the church or law. Beyond the rudiments of reading, writing and arithmetic, some of the best minds in the colonies may be said to have educated themselves through reading, and it was within the capabilities of men like Franklin and Jefferson to attempt to master all knowledge, as far as it went in the eighteenth century.

One step down the social ladder, though down more often because of financial rating than because of birth, were the merchants. In a country where practically everyone was in mercantile business to some degree, it was the Scotsmen who called themselves " merchants." These men had fled the old country largely for political reasons, had finally taken the oath abjuring the Pretenders, and had become an economic power in the colony. The British Navigation Acts imposed a devastating tax on all goods sold to other countries and decreed that they must first pass through an English port to have this tax collected. The Scottish ports, on the other hand, extended a hearty welcome to all American ships that carried cargoes destined for the continent, and helped them evade the port laws. Glasgow became one of the great ports of the eighteenth century and branches of Scottish business houses appeared along the Virginia rivers. Alexandria, Colchester, Dumfries, Fredericksburg,

Tappahannock and Petersburg were all dominated by these excellent business men who managed to combine their native astuteness with the more liberal and pleasure-loving code of the English colonists. It was not long before they were building race-tracks and theatres and holding a social season that outdistanced that of the Crown officials in Williamsburg. It was not long either before they married into the old established families, became property owners, vestrymen and justices.

William Buckland left the comforts of his uncle's home to join a vast army of artisans and laborers which made up nearly two-thirds of the population of colonial America.[5] The early colonists were, as might be expected, in constant need of workmen. Whether they had gone to America for adventure or escape, most were not skilled craftsmen nor were they prepared for the hard life of settlers. In order to exist they must perforce turn farmer and before that could be done the primeval forests must be felled and shelters built. The extremes of the climate, particularly the heat of Virginia summers and the prevalence of malaria, discouraged many an ardent colonist.

By 1750 the colonists were so desperate for laborers that few questions were asked in regard to background or training. A planter could buy a laborer or craftsman for four years' use for as little as £10 or as much as £75. The prospective immigrant on the other hand often discovered that he had jumped from the frying-pan into the fire and found his fate in the new world little better than that which he had left behind.

There were, of course, many Europeans emigrating who had the means to pay their own passage but they did not lessen the labor shortage. In a short time they in turn wanted servants of their own and wrote "gent." after their names. The system of indenture was the common method of supplying the commodity so much in demand and which existed in large supply in England.

These "indentured servants" came from all classes. Often they were relatives of the colonists, or carefully chosen for some special skill or trade. They were younger sons of the gentry with no future at home; they were orphans, they were the unfortunates and sometimes the dregs of a pitiless society. To pay for their passage to new opportunities they bound themselves to work for an unknown master. He in turn promised them food, drink, clothes and in rare instances a cash allowance.

It was a contract for mutual helpfulness. The contract was not unlike that for apprentices, but the master promised no educational benefits and the courts assumed much less jurisdiction over the welfare of these adults. The " servant " had to keep the written agreement upon his person at all times and when his term was up the other half of the indenture was restored to him. It was his only means of identification, and forging papers constituted a high crime.

The people who had been hired in England and were assured of positions in the colonies fared well, that is, if they worked hard and had the skills they professed. Unfortunately, the greatest demand was always for countrymen who could level the forests and till the soil, and few of the city men could last out their four years at this arduous work. Runaway servants were the inevitable result, a cause for extra laws, crowded courts and columns of advertising in the local newspapers.

The " servants " who were brought as cargo by ship captains or by those in the business of recruiting labor had a harder fate. When volunteers were not produced in sufficient number the British government contracted to empty the overcrowded prisons. Abuses were frequent. As cargoes these unfortunates were crowded on ships and disposed of by sale at the dock as advantageously to the importer as possible. Convict laborers did not expect to find life any easier, for they had chosen to live rather than be hanged.

What chance then did a " free-willer," as those who paid their own passage were called, with neither family connections nor money behind him have to earn a living and to break into the closed circle of colonial society? He could perform menial work for a planter, be store-boy to a merchant, take up a trade in one of the growing towns, or shoulder an axe or a gun in the unsurveyed forest. If he were diligent and healthy he might eventually own land, or a schooner, and become a tobacco merchant on his own. With twenty-five acres and a homestead he was entitled to vote, even if he could neither read nor write, a defect which in a few cases did not hinder a man from being elected to a vestry.

By 1755 the old lines between social and economic groups were dissolving in a wave of native enthusiasm for the political rights of man. The " melting pot " was already simmering. Men capable of guiding the destinies of a new nation were being bred by farmers, printers, merchants and by indentured servants. Women were held more strictly to their own social strata by the obvious difficulty of travel and intimacy with others in an outside world. Men vastly predominated in the population so that there were few unmarried women. The size of dowries had definite appeal, however, to their wooers and there was little compunction in taking marriage as a business matter.

Neighborhood sociability and unlimited hospitality were universally practiced in Virginia where country houses were large, servants plentiful and distances great. Washington once compared Mount Vernon to "a well resorted tavern" and noted that on one occasion only he dined alone with his wife.[6]

There were inns to be sure, some very good ones. Travelers in the colony about this time remarked that inns were called ordinaries in the southern colonies. "The Inns are very different from those in Europe; the master and mistress sit down at the table with you, do the honors of a good meal and in leaving you pay without haggling."[7] These inns were on the post-roads and catered to the burgesses enroute to Williamsburg. The inns at Dumfries, Colchester and Alexandria did a thriving business because the roads were often so bad as to be impassable. The mail frequently could not go through to the South and passengers were forced to abandon coach and chaise when they were mired in attempting to skirt the heads of rivers. One woman traveler is quoted as saying "The Roads are so Bad that I am almost disjointed."[8]

In this environment the owner of Gunston Hall grew up. Like many other families of Tidewater Virginia the Masons had come to America with the supporters of Charles II after September, 1651, when they had lost the last battle of the English Civil War.[9] Two years previous, in 1649, the year of the first Charles' execution, it is said that one ship alone brought over 350 royalists. The great grandfather of George Mason, one of the royalist refugees, patented land in March, 1655, "for transportation of eighteen persons into the colony." Much additional land was acquired by him as well as by succeeding generations of men high in the government of the colony, so that George Mason IV was among the large landholders. His plantation of Woodbridge included the ownership of the ferry across Occoquan Creek, important as being part of the highway to the South. He also held by inheritance farms in other counties as well as over the Potomac in Maryland, but not content with his cultivated acres, he was through the years buying western lands to develop.

George Mason III had chosen to live in Maryland. On one of his routine crossings of the Potomac river his boat capsized and he was drowned. This tragic event caused his widow to return to Virginia with her three small children. Ann Thomson Mason was the daughter of a distinguished attorney general and in her own right a woman of force and character. She could not have been so successful in the up-bringing of her children, however, if she had not had the help of their other guardian, John Mercer of Marlborough, Stafford County. Mercer, who had married a Mason aunt, was a man of great ability and wisdom but so hot-tempered that for a time he was forbidden to practice law. It was during this period of enforced quiescence that he devoted his time, energy and excellent library to the Mason children.

The elder son, George, inherited all his father's estate. He studied law but his heart was set on becoming a successful planter. When he reached his majority he left his mother's home to take over the oldest Mason plantation, Dogue's Neck, higher up the Potomac River in what was to become the new county of Fairfax. The Maryland land was also under his supervision and soon he renewed a childhood friendship with a neighbor on an estate adjoining his Stump Neck in Charles County. On April 4, 1750, George Mason and Ann Eilbeck were married. It was about this time that Hesselius, the Maryland artist, painted the likenesses of the bride and groom. Ann's auburn hair is set off by a blue silk dress, while George is painted in brown velvet coat and yellow satin waistcoat. As Hesselius never flattered his subjects, we can surmise that the bride was really pretty and that the plump groom was handsome, with lively dark eyes and prominent eyebrows. Straight and athletic though he is reputed to have been, he was afflicted all through his life by that eighteenth century crippler, gout, which at times left him bedridden and often able to move only with crutches.

The second Mason son, Thomson, who was William Buckland's guide to America, had, as we have seen, been educated in law at the Inns of Court. He was to become the most eminent lawyer of his time in Virginia. As one of only a dozen or so barristers trained in England, his practice grew rapidly both at Dumfries and at Williamsburg, until he later became judge of the court in Loudoun County. In 1758 he, too, renewed his ties with Maryland and there married Mary Barnes, daughter of Abraham Barnes, probably the most prominent citizen of

Southern Maryland. Like all young couples, they wished a home of their own but for two years continued to live with old Mrs. Mason at Chappawamsic. From Stafford County Thomson was elected to the Assembly in 1759. Since he and his sister Ann, wife of Major Samuel Selden of Salvington, had been left nothing under the law of primogeniture, their mother, with great business acumen, bought " wild lands " for them in the newly formed Loudoun County and thither the young couple eventually went to live.

It was a compact little world in which they all moved. Life centered around the county courthouses, the parish churches, the river shipping and the local stores. Business was discussed over pipes and brandy in taverns or in the offices of the country gentlemen's estates, and business was the reason more often than sociability when George Mason put up an acquaintance for the night. Merchant though every American was at heart, politics and sometimes adventure were also a part of his makeup.

The opening of the western lands was more than a vision to George Mason and to his neighbor George Washington. Many a visitor to Dogue's Neck or Mount Vernon was bent on promoting the canal on the Potomac River or expanding the iron foundry at Occoquan or in building a grist mill. Tobacco was everybody's business.

The election of burgesses qualified to carry out the wishes of the landed class was of vital interest to the gentry. " The middling sort " relied on their superiors to look out for their needs until such time as their own ambitions could be gratified. " The inferior sort " had no say whatsoever. The same few men held all the local governmental offices but took their positions of responsibility with great seriousness. Thus George Mason served on the Fairfax County Court as a justice, as a vestryman of the parish, as a trustee of Colchester and of the larger town Alexandria, and as commissary to Braddock's troops quartered in Alexandria. He was active in the promotion of justice, mercy, charity, and all neighborhood improvements. But politics, per se, had no fascination for either of the Mason brothers. One term in the Assembly in 1759 brought George to the realization that both time and money were wasted and that he could better achieve his ends by working behind the scenes. Years later when he wrote his will he admonished his children " to prefer the happiness of independence and a private station to the troubles and vexations of public business." However, his advice was eagerly sought and freely given, whether on the subject of propagating fruit trees or on expressing those ideals of human rights and liberty which were but incoherent visions in the minds of other men. He possessed the complete confidence of the political leaders and through them he disseminated his own ideas.

There was, however, a lighter side to George Mason's nature which showed itself occasionally. He was considered one of the best shots in the country-side and with his deer park and large acres, he often held hunts for invited guests. Colonel Sharpe, Governor of Maryland, Colonel William Fairfax, Colonel Washington, Colonel Blackburn of Rippon Lodge and others joined him in the winter season. When his gout progressed to a chronic stage he had to forego this, his one sporting pleasure. But his library was always a resource and his intimate friends came often to his fireside to enjoy his stimulating conversation; Daniel McCarty, a fellow vestryman; the Hendersons, merchant and barrister; Hector Ross, a fellow justice; most of them Scotsmen. Martin Cockburn of Springfield had married a Mason cousin and since they had no children of their own, they became deputy parents to George Mason's flock. Springfield was within walking distance, with Cedar Grove of the McCarty's just north of it and the Fairfaxes' Belvoir was on the next point of the river, a mere ten minutes' boat ride. Beyond Belvoir lay Colonel Washington's Mount Vernon.[10]

This midcentury Virginia greeted young Buckland with a certain complacency. People were accustomed to continuing streams of new arrivals and they, like all countrymen, were intent on what their own day brought forth. Was it going to rain? Has Hector Ross's *Jeanie* docked, and have my hogsheads been inspected and passed? What dispatches from the war has this week's *Gazette?* Are the Iroquois on our side or with the French? The young joiner could tell them only the latest London news. It would be months before he could join in their local discussions.

III

Gunston Hall

THE YOUNG George Masons of Dogue's Neck began to find their inherited quarters cramped and old-fashioned. Their eldest child was born in 1753 and shortly thereafter they picked out a site for a new house.[1] This site was still on the two thousand acre plantation, still on the Potomac River, slightly to the north. By placing the new house at the point of the peninsula a beautiful view could be had up and down the river and across to the Maryland shore. Mason decided to call this part of his estate Gunston after his maternal grandmother's place in Charles County, Maryland. That earlier Gunston had, in turn, been named for her grandfather Fowke's Staffordshire estate, and thus the fifth generation repeated the English designation.

Building a mansion in the colonies was a serious undertaking. It was discussed with neighbors. Architectural books such as Swan's *British Architecture* or James Gibbs' works were bought and studied. The prevailing winds and soil composition must be considered. But it was a form of creative work and expression which every gentleman felt qualified to attempt, some with more success than others. Thomas Jefferson in his *Notes on the State of Virginia* took a dim view of the contemporary scene:

> The private buildings are very rarely constructed of stone or brick; much the greatest portion being of scantling and boards, plaistered with lime. It is impossible to devise things more ugly, uncomfortable, and happily more perishable. There are two or three plans, on one of which, according to its size, most of the houses in the state are built . . . A workman could scarcely be found here capable of drawing an order. . . . The genius of architecture seems

22

to have shed its maledictions over this land . . . The unhappy prejudice prevails that houses of brick or stone are less wholesome than those of wood.[2]

Despite Mr. Jefferson, the houses of the great plantation owners showed their British inheritance with minor concessions to climate and avail-

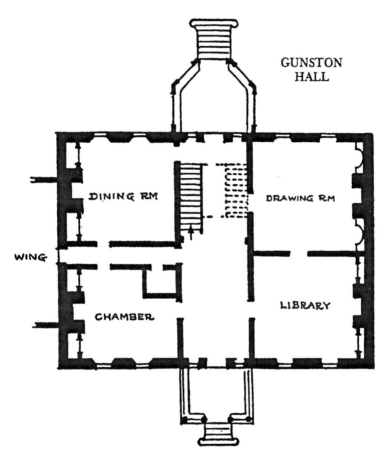

GUNSTON
HALL

DINING RM

DRAWING RM

WING

CHAMBER

LIBRARY

able materials. But if the theory were mastered there was still the practical application of it to surmount. A master craftsman who had learned his trade in England was a rarity in mid-eighteenth century Virginia. Mason determined that such a man he must find and employ if his Gunston Hall were to become a reality. We have seen that this desire was gratified with the arrival in the fall of 1755 of William Buckland.

It is almost certain that the plan of the house had been determined upon and that the brick walls were erected by the time Mason felt the need of an experienced man to complete the interior details. The very wording of the recommendation endorsed on the back of Buckland's indenture, " having had the entire Direction of the Carpenters and Joiners work," leads one to believe that the planning and masonry work had already been completed. It also intimates that Buckland himself did very little, if any, manual labor. He had the entire direction of Mason's slaves and of other indentured servants and what a trial it must have been! General Washington once wrote of his own Negro carpenters: " There is not to be found so idle a set of Rascalls." Instead of the well trained and experienced men that Buckland was accustomed to see working for his uncle in London, he was given spot-trained Negroes, convicts who preferred the building trades to work in the fields, and perhaps a native journeyman or two. When it came to carving the intricate designs for the interior woodwork, only an experienced hand could have been employed. Perhaps this was the young Londoner's personal contribution. Mason asserted further in his indorsement: " I think [him] a complete Master of the Carpenter's and Joiner's.Business both in theory and practice." [3] Theory would be the design, practice the actual carving. The carved work on mantels, cupboards, cornices and chair-rails puts Gunston in a class of its own as the most elaborate of any contemporary house in the middle colonies, more so than any of Buckland's subsequent work.

For the first year the young joiner and his workmen were probably housed at the Dogue's Neck estate from which, by a short ride each day, they would be at their place of employment. The outbuildings, or at least some of them, were certain to be the first built so they could be used before the great house was ready for occupancy. Since George Mason was a meticulous caretaker of his estate and a perfectionist in everything he did, one can be sure that he kept a close watch on his joiner and discussed every detail with him. In his voluminous correspondence there is but one reference to his building. It is a letter written some years later to an intimate friend. He warns him against the porosity of salmon brick and gives his receipt for mortar.

When I built my House I was at pains to measure all the Lime and Sand as my Mortar was made up and always had two Beds, one for

outside-work ⅔ Lime and ⅓ Sand, the other equal parts of Lime
and Sand for Inside-work . . . it is easily measured in any Tub or
Barrel, and there is no other way to be sure of having your mortar
good without waste, and the different parts of Yr Building equally
strong. . . . If you have any good pit sand, out of your Cellars or
well, it will make your mortar much tougher and stronger. . . .
Next to pit sand the River Shoar Sand on fresh water is best and
the Sand in the road worst of all; as being very foul and full of Dust.

I wou'd by no means put any Clay or Loam in any of the
Mortar, in the first place the mortar is not near so strong and
besides from its being of a more soft and crumbly nature, it is very
apt to nourish and harbour those pernicious little vermin the
Cockroaches . . . and this I assure you is no slight Consideration;
for I have seen some brick Houses so infested with these Devils
that a Man had better have lived in a Barne than in one of them.[4]

The only firsthand family description of Gunston Hall was written
years after the building, by the youngest of George Mason's sons. It
shows how varied were the structures on a plantation and with what
care Mason laid out his gardens and orchards.

Gunston Hall is situated on a height on the right bank of the
Potomac river within a short walk of the shores, and commanding
a full view of it. . . . When I can first remember it, it was in a state
of high improvement and carefully kept. The south front looked
to the river; from an elevated little portico on this front you de-
scended directly into an extensive garden.

Then follows a lengthy description of the north, or approach front with
its avenue of four rows of cherry trees. The description continues:—

To the west of the main building were first the schoolhouse, and
then at a little distance, masked by a row of large English walnut
trees, were the stables. To the east was a high paled yard, adjoining the house, into which opened an outer door from the private
front, within, or connected with which yard were the kitchen, well,
poultry houses and other domestic arrangements; and beyond it
on the same side, were the corn house and granary, servants houses
(in those days called negro quarters) hay yard and cattle pens,
all of which were masked by rows of large cherry and mulberry
trees. And adjoining the enclosed grounds on which stood the
mansion and all these appendages on the eastern side was an extensive pasture for stock of all kinds running down to the river,
through which led the road to the Landing . . . where all persons

or things water borne, were landed or taken off, and where were kept the boats, pettiaugers and canoes of which there were always several for business transportation, fishing and hunting . . . The west side of the lawn . . . was skirted by a wood, just far enough within which to be out of sight, was a little village called Log Town . . . built of hewn pine logs. Here lived . . . my father's body-servant James . . . and those of several negro carpenters.

It was very much the practise with gentlemen of landed and slave estates in the interior of Virginia, so to organize them as to have considerable resources within themselves; to employ . . . but few tradesmen and to buy little or none of the coarse stuffs and materials used by them. . . . Thus my father had among his slaves carpenters, coopers, sawyers, blacksmiths, tanners, curriers, shoe-makers, spinners, weavers and knitters, and even a distiller. His woods furnished timber and plank for the carpenters and coopers. . . . His carpenters and sawyers built and kept in repair all the dwellinghouses, barns, stables . . . and the outhouses at the home house.[5]

Gunston Hall is by no means a pretentious house commensurate with the wealth and position of its builder. It is one story brick in Flemish bond with sandstone trim and modillioned wood cornice. Bedrooms lighted by dormers are within the roof construction and two chimneys are located at each of the gable ends. The corners of the brick walls are strengthened and decorated by Aquia Creek quoins from the famous quarry down river, whence the stones were probably transported by barge to Gunston wharf. The same stone, forty years later, was sent up river to Washington for the construction of the Executive Mansion.

The design of Gunston is very like, not only nearby Wakefield, the birthplace of George Washington, but the original Mount Vernon before its enlargement. Both houses were undoubtedly well known to George Mason. The plan was usual in the middle colonies—hall extending front to back, accommodating the stair, principal rooms in the four corners. A variation at Gunston is a narrow corridor between the two rooms on the east side that led to services that no longer exist.

All Gunston details are well within the Georgian tradition that contemporary taste required and that Buckland by training was capable of providing. They are perhaps the most ornate of any of the colonial houses of Virginia and they testify to the owner's delight in richness of detail and his willingness to give the skill of his joiner full play. Except for the low wainscot on the stair, there is no paneling. The wood walls were intended to be covered with some sort of fabric. Wood cornices, chair rails, base boards, mantels and over-doors are elaborately carved. The doorways and niches at each side of the chimney breasts are surmounted by broken pediments. It might be noted that the doors are unusually low. An explanation is difficult to come by. Perhaps they are low to conserve heat in occupied rooms.

The stair hall is similar to that at Mount Vernon except that the division between the entrance hall and the stair hall is marked by two elliptical arches separated by a pendentive in the form of a pineapple, since Roman times a symbol of hospitality. The keystone of these arches breaks through the bed mould of the cornice. Buckland was to repeat these arches later at Montpelier and Tulip Hill in Maryland. Balusters, only two to the tread, are turned. There is ample evidence in door trim and over-doors that Buckland had not yet assimilated the lessons in the pattern books nor reached the assurance and full maturity that he was to display later in Annapolis.

The two porches, one at the entrance and the other overlooking the garden and the distant Potomac, are well proportioned and delightfully designed and executed. The entrance porch displays the conventional Doric triglyphs and guttae and a skillful use of an arch breaking through the entablature in the Palladian manner. The five-sided porch that leads to the garden has unexpected pointed arches in combination with the semi-circular one of classic tradition. The combination however, was not unknown in the eighteenth century in England, and a book known to have been in Buckland's library at the time of his death, Batty Langley's *Gothic Architecture*, published in London in 1747, illustrates Gothic and Classic details in combination. Even Chippendale's book of furniture shows not infrequently the same combination, and Gibbs' *Book of Architecture*, so influential among eighteenth century designers, is not without Gothic motives. The Chinese ornaments in the dining room are more difficult to trace. The Chinese vogue in building and decoration commenced when the English architect, William Chambers, returned from China and by his notes influenced Chippendale and other designers. It may well be that Buckland, before he finished his work at Gunston—he worked for George Mason as late as 1761—had seen Chambers' book, *Designs of Chinese Buildings, Furniture, Dresses, Etc.* (London, 1757), and obtained suggestions from it. However, it must be recorded that an effort to trace the derivations of particular details employed by the designers working in colonial America is in most cases pointless. They are almost always the accepted idiom of the times. They were repeated endlessly in hundreds of town and country houses in England and are to be found in the architectural books published in great numbers which were popular among the owners of estates.

It took nearly four years to complete Gunston Hall. William Buckland was not as lonely as might be expected. His companions on the plantation were farm overseers, the children's schoolmaster, visiting farmers and merchants of what Dr. Hamilton of Annapolis called " the middling sort." [6] He had a room in a building sometime later to be the schoolhouse, furnished in country style with bed, stool and table. At least it gave him privacy, where he could work on his sketches and plans by the light of two candles. Here were all his worldly possessions, his little trunk holding his superior English-made clothes, his few books and drawing instruments, and here he could entertain a friend before a log fire with an evening of conversation over a glass of rum punch or " cyder."

There were days when work on the house was impossible; materials not ready, weather too cold, or an important craftsman laid up with fever. Squire Mason, well-known as a kind master, probably did not hold his young joiner too strictly to the law of indentureship. When the racing season was on in the spring and fall the whole countryside took to the road leading to the nearest track, whether interested in horseflesh or not. [7] Sociability was sufficient reason to go to Bogges' track (now the seat of Pohick Church) or to beg a lift to the larger race grounds at Alexandria. Some days Buckland could get to Colchester to bring back small purchases made at the three thriving stores full of newly imported goods of Messrs. Hector Ross, Alexander Henderson or John Glassford & Co. [8] In Colchester he could hear all the local news and criticism of the army in its losing fight against the French. If he wanted to find a relaxed and garrulous traveler who could give him news of London or the world beyond Virginia, he would go to the taproom of " The Arms of Fairfax." This hostelry was so nearly up to the best English standard that it drew praise from the most critical of visitors.[9]

And then there were Sundays. George Mason was a vestryman of Truro Parish, and undoubtedly saw to it that his household arrived on time for the Sunday service, weather permitting. The old frame Pohick Church which Colonel Washington did not feel was worth repair for it was not centrally located, stood at the Occoquan ferry, convenient to Dogue's Neck, a mere two-mile ride.

In the neighborhood of the old church lived William Moore, with his wife, three daughters and two sons, on a plantation on Accotink Creek, an estuary of Gunston Cove. In 1727 Moore patented his dwelling plantation of 500 acres, and he worked, besides this land, another plantation rented from George Mason.[10] Little is known of Moore except that he was a Processioner chosen to beat the bounds of Truro Parish, an office given only to those of some standing in the church and community.[11] He predeceased his wife, Mary, by four years, having previously written a will that divided his original holdings among his children either as dowries or gifts. William Moore was not a great landholder but one of the smaller planters. He worked his farms with the help of five slaves, and after a residence in Virginia of approximately forty-two years, left to his wife an estate of £459. To daughter Sarah and her husband, Marcelus Littlejohn, had been given a farm on the Ox Road, while the eldest son, James, received 200 acres of the original patent. The youngest daughter, Ann, made the best match for she became the bride of Charles Tyler of Cameron Parish, a churchwarden and one of the gentlemen justices of the newly formed Loudoun County. The middle daughter fell in love with the penniless young William Buckland just starting on a career.[12]

An indentured servant was forbidden to marry without the consent of his master, but there were no rules against meeting the opposite sex in church. A kind master would have allowed a home visit now and then, provided it did not interfere with work, and might even bestow his blessing on the romance. Planter Moore was possibly more ambitious for his daughter, but on the other hand, he probably sympathized with a young man of talent and good yeoman stock. It is certain that the young people had had time to know each other well before Buckland left the employ of George Mason.

The date the Masons moved into their new house is clearly defined. The first two of their twelve children were born at Dogue's Neck but the family Bible records the birth of the third son at Gunston in 1759. George Mason used his Gunston Hall address for the first time after May, 1758. This would seem to prove that the new mansion was by that time livable. It goes without saying that all the plantation buildings were not completed. A plantation, like any good garden, is never entirely completed, and George Mason, good gardener that he was, certainly planted and moved, built and rebuilt for the rest of his life.

Late in 1759 William Buckland's term of servitude was completed. He was twenty-five years old and there were three choices he could make as to his future. If he had saved enough from his small salary for passage home, he could have returned to England; he could apply for a grant to western lands and settle as a backwoodsman; or he could set himself up in his profession among the rich planters of Virginia. He had made his choice of a wife and he now decided to cast his lot permanently in the new world. His only assets were his skill, his good looks and the endorsement given him by a satisfied employer. On the 8th of November, on the back of the 1755 indenture, the squire of Gunston Hall wrote:

> The within named William Buckland came into Virginia with my brother Thomson Mason, who engaged him in London, and had a very good Character of him there; during the time he lived with me he had the entire Direction of the Carpenters and Joiners work of a large House; and having behaved very faithfully in my service, I can with great justice recommend him . . . as an honest sober diligent man & I think a complete Master of the Carpenter's and Joiner's Business both in theory and practice.[13]

This was high praise from any man, but from George Mason it carried added weight. With his papers in his pocket and on a horse of his own, he probably rode directly to claim the hand of his fair neighbor, Mary Moore. There can be no doubt of the identity of William Buckland's wife, for though she appears in her father's will and again in her mother's as " Mary Bucklin," Mary Moore Buckland is written clearly with her dates in an old Irish Book of Common Prayer handed down through generations of the Mann family, her descendants.[14] There are no existing marriage records in the county for this period and circumstantial evidence points to 1759 as the year of the wedding. Buckland was free to marry and had promises of employment. On his Colchester store account there is the record of his having purchased at this time " one necklace, a bridle," and sufficient rum to have provided cheer at a feast.[15] However, the Mann family records place the marriage in 1758, which was, of course, possible with Mason's consent.

Two commissions for building awaited the bridegroom immediately, both in the neighborhood and both procured through his association with George Mason. It is reasonable to suppose that William and Mary lived with the Moores on Accotink Creek until this work was finished. Further items on his 1760 store account of " one pair of knitting needles " and large quantities of ribbon point directly to feminine diversion. As William Moore later, in his will, bequeathed no land to his daughter Mary, but cut her off with her sisters at one shilling apiece, though Sarah and Ann had each an earlier gift of land, it seems probable that he advanced a sum of money to her as dowry. In 1759 Buckland was in desperate need of both cash and credit to set himself up as a master-builder with skilled indentured servants of his own.

With whatever help he had, he undertook with enthusiasm his first personal commission, that of building the new glebe house for Falls Church in Truro Parish. Property had been acquired on the stage road between Alexandria and Colchester for the Reverend Charles Green, long rector of this parish with its three scattered churches and congregations. The glebe-house was to be of brick, one story with cellar and convenient closets. Thomas Waite of the parish had been given the contract as early as 1752 but neglected his work or did it so poorly that the patience of the vestry was quite exhausted seven years later. William Buckland was then engaged to complete the building and to receive the £425 promised to Waite.[16]

At this same time a larger residence with more outlet for the imagination fell to his lot.[17] One of Mason's friends and business associates, John Ballendine, decided to move from Prince William County nearer to his flour and grist mills and his iron foundry, at the falls of the Occoquan. Ballendine was a promoter with no capital. Being self-made, he sought the balanced judgment of George Mason for his various enterprises and was a frequent visitor to Gunston Hall. He is described as

" a picturesque figure " and certainly he chose a picturesque spot in which to build his home.

The lot on which the house stands is carved out of a rocky ledge and overlooks a beautiful woodland slope on the far side of a gorge through which run the falls. A quarry on the creek supplied stone for the mansion and Mason's highly recommended builder supplied plans and workmen. It is a simple house, not one in which Buckland could use to advantage his London-trained skills. But perched on a crag, high above the roaring falls and the ruins of eighteenth century industry, it surveys the romantic scene with a certain dignity. Stone houses are unusual in Tidewater Virginia and this one is built in three parts. The main block is a two-story structure, one room deep, with gable roof. Two wings on the same side suggest that the smaller was the first built. This part still contains great ovens where the local flour was baked into loaves for commercial use. The house contains simple but good woodwork consisting of six conventional mantels, chair rails, base boards and cornices in the principal rooms. There is a handsome dentilled cornice on the exterior. Below Rockledge, as Ballendine called it, small terraces are cut into the cliff where, today, hollyhocks and Sweet William bloom. Here and at Gunston men with vision sat before wide fireplaces talking far into the night of navigating the Potomac to bring the great Western Lands nearer, for Ballendine, George Mason, George Washington, Robert Carter, and William Fitzhugh were all associated in the Potomac Canal project.

On these two houses Buckland spent the years 1760 and 1761. As the plantation buildings at Gunston were not entirely completed he had to return there at times to supervise the work of a journeyman or apprentice, left behind.[18] By 1762 he was once more free to seek employment and to go where opportunity offered.

There were capable men in the colony ahead of him who were building the new towns of Alexandria and Fredericksburg. Dumfries was closer to his base and some architects have thought that Buckland must have had a hand in certain buildings there. The town was important enough in 1759 to become the seat of Prince William County and boasted a new courthouse and many handsome dwellings. But with the silting of the river, this town, like Colchester, all but disappeared. In recent times but two examples of eighteenth-century brick architecture in Dumfries survived and now only the old tavern is left. This house, as was the demolished Tebbs house, is built with all header bond, a form of brick work seldom used in England or in Virginia but common in Annapolis. Good cornices and distinguished interior wood-work mark it as the work of an experienced craftsman.

It would seem most probable that if and when Thomson Mason built himself a house he would have employed the young joiner who had accompanied him from England. Two years after his marriage he left his mother's plantation and went to live in Loudoun County on an estate purchased years before as an investment. On this estate, Rasp-berry Plains, stood a house built either by the original grantee in 1731 or by the second owner, a blacksmith.[19] We can be sure that it was a simple affair, suited to life in the backwoods. However, Loudoun County was fast being populated by a third generation of the blood and wealth of Stafford, Fairfax, Prince William and the lower counties. The land was exceedingly fertile and the climate healthy.

It is hard to believe that this distinguished and hospitable man, later a Judge, continued to live with his wife in a primitive, unattractive dwelling. A new brick Raspberry Plains, complete with one wing, a handsome doorway and a bullseye window in the pediment was built, either by Thomson Mason or his son. A reliable authority has given the date 1771 to this house.[20] If this date is correct, Buckland could well have been the architect for his first American friend. However, an existing document has clouded the certainty of this statement. In the 1803 will of Thomson Mason's son, Stevens Thomson Mason, there is the baffling clause that he wished his heirs to complete " a house now building." Unfortunately the second Raspberry Plains burned many years ago, which leaves only an early photograph for the record. It has been replaced by still another house on the same site. It is still quite possible that by 1771, or even earlier, Thomson Mason finished his Raspberry Plains, and that the son's house was elsewhere on the prop-erty. There is no way known at the present time to establish the facts. What seemed such an excellent lead to another Buckland building must remain unsolved.

IV

Richmond County

THE TIME had come when the young joiner, now a master builder, was forced once again to make some decision as to his future. Opportunity beckoned one hundred miles away in what is known as the Northern Neck, that narrow peninsula between the Potomac and the Rappahannock rivers. The most plausible reason for the move from a section of Virginia that had been his home for over six years is that he availed himself of the chance to work with an already established architect, John Ariss. Ariss, also known as Ayres and Oriss, advertised in the *Maryland Gazette* on May 22, 1751, that he was living at Bushfield, the home of Major John Bushrod in Westmoreland County, and was prepared to do business. The notice read:

> Buildings of all Sorts and Dimensions are undertaken; . . . ancient or modern Order of Gibbs' Architecture, plans,—Draughts may be seen and sundry buildings near finished after modern taste.

Ariss had prominent friends and connections. His father was of Westmoreland County and is reported to have been a builder. Apparently Ariss had had formal training, though we know not where. Through his ability and his patrons he received commissions to inspect the construction of Cople Church in 1753 and to draw plans for Payne's Church in Truro Parish in 1776 and for other churches later in Berkeley County (now West Virginia). This promising architect disappears from Northern Neck records after 1762 but appears in those of Berkeley County in 1772. From 1792 he was a tenant until his death in 1799 on one of George Washington's estates.[1]

34

In 1762 Ariss was buying land in Richmond County, so it is probable that he stayed on there for a few more years in the neighborhood of what is now the town of Warsaw and that William Buckland arrived there to work with him. On a rented plantation near the same crossroads, at that time called Richmond Court House, also lived a man who had undoubtedly known of Buckland at Gunston, for he was an intimate friend of George Mason's. This was Daniel French, Gent., of Rose Hill, Fairfax County, a wealthy planter and vestryman of Truro Parish.[2] His avocation was building and he was "undertaker" of various public buildings, such as jails and churches. An architect, a contractor and William Buckland all living within a stone's throw of one another suggests that they may have combined their resources.

The third generation of colonial planters with good tobacco credits in England and loans at interest in the colonies demanded a comfortable life comparable with that of country gentlemen in England. They were, therefore, enlarging their mansions to be in the latest fashion. French and Buckland undoubtedly came to this section of Virginia to assist in some construction of Ariss' design and promotion.

The earliest documentary evidence of the arrival of the Bucklands in Richmond County is found in the Court Records for June, 1762, a case in which William is assignee for a Francis Moore.[3] This may have been a family duty for some relative of his in-laws. Undoubtedly, however, George Mason's endorsement had preceded him and this would have been sufficient introduction to the powerful Carter and Tayloe families, who owned a large part of the county's fertile fields, controlled the courts and parishes and had the patronage of contracts for all public works.

Colonel Landon Carter lived at his seat Sabine Hall on one side of the King's Highway and Colonel John Tayloe resided in grandeur at Mount Airy on the other side. Both estates were but a mile or two from the Court House, both were on eminences overlooking the Rappahannock opposite Hobbes' Hole (Tappahannock). Landon Carter was the son of "King" Carter, agent for Culpeper and Fairfax, proprietors of the Northern Neck. By this portfolio "King" Carter had become the wealthiest man in his era. His grandsons were increasing the prestige of the family and two of them lived near by, Robert Wormeley at Sabine Hall with his father and Councillor Robert, when not on duty in Williamsburg, at Nomini Hall, an estate but a few miles the other side of the Court House. Colonel Tayloe was allied with most of the " Court Circle " of Maryland and had a bevy of attractive daughters who eventually became the mistresses of other great Virginia estates. The breeding and racing of horses was his great diversion from the arduous duties of serving as judge of the Petty Court and of managing his plantations. William Buckland crossed the paths of these two great nabobs many times.

Sabine Hall had been completed well before Buckland's arrival in Richmond County. The date usually given for the building of Mount Airy is 1758. But there is very good circumstantial evidence that work continued on the mansion and that the hand that did the interior wood-work was that of the carver of Gunston Hall.[4]

Mount Airy was the most ambitious house to be built in Virginia. Its terraced gardens, overlooking the valley of the Rappahanock River, contained an orangerie and bowling green, and the surrounding deer park gave it a truly English character. The house is constructed of local brown stone with cut limestone string courses, trim and quoins. The central block is connected to square wings by quarter-circle enclosed passageways. Unity is achieved in the spreading composition by the skillful relation of the parts and the same hip roof that crowns each element. The tall chimneys rise from the main block on each side of the architectural feature that expresses on the façade the central hall, and from the square wings at the center of the roof. Throughout his career Buckland drew inspiration from Gibbs' *Book of Architecture*, which he used as a source. At Mount Airy the plan is similar to many shown in this book and later in Annapolis he was to use doorways, mantels, window treatments and minor architectural details from it. A fragment of cornice surviving the disastrous fire of 1844 shows a marked similarity to corresponding details at Gunston. But even more convincing that the wood carver and designer was none other than Buckland is the following extract from one of Colonel Tayloe's neighborly notes to his elderly and contentious friend, Landon Carter, written October 16, 1762, ". . . and if you would ride to Mt. Airy sometimes and give your friendly hints of admonition to Mr. Buckland I believe it would be doing me no small service." [5] Here is assurance that the recently arrived joiner was hard at work at Mount Airy and how disappointing it is that the results of this labor, presumably the interior woodwork, was so long ago destroyed. Business between Buckland and the Tayloes continued through the years. The Colonel went security for him in a law suit in 1763 and in another letter to Landon Carter, dated January 3, 1768, he mentions " 8 chairs and 2 elbow ones that are in Buckland's hands to sell." [6]

The year 1763 placed on permanent record one of the most interesting clues to Buckland's previous years. A journeyman, James Brent, brought suit in the Richmond County court against Buckland for sums he considered due him during his three and a half years' employment.[7] Each side prepared statements without benefit of counsel, containing detailed entries for clothing, wages, rum, levy and poll tax, cash borrowed for an October race, covering a mare, and lastly for work done for various employers. It is in this Brent account that we find proof that Buckland worked for Major Samuel Selden, George Mason's brother-in-law, proof that he was intimate enough with Bernard Sears, joiner and carver, to buy him a pair of shoes; and that Brent was left behind at Gunston Hall where he put in more than a year's work at one shilling per day. Dr. Nesbit, the good Colchester doctor, was paid eight shillings, nine pence, for medical attentions and sundries were bought by Buckland at Hector Ross's store at Colchester. James Brent's salary increased from ten pounds in 1759 to forty-five shillings a month or twenty seven pounds for the year 1763. If Brent had been an apprentice he probably could not have been left behind at Colonel Mason's, and yet the account shows a sort of paternal housekeeping for the young man. Since Brent had his expenses paid from Richmond County to Fairfax only a month after Buckland had become independent, either Richmond was his home or he was down the Northern Neck on Buckland's business. The two contestants had no trouble in agreeing on the " Account of time " but the sundries defy any accountant but an eighteenth century Gentleman Justice! The Court decreed that William Buckland owed Brent £15 17s 5d.

A man may live his life without blemish, love his wife, pay his bills, mind his own business and when his generation has passed be known but to God. If, however, he gets himself into a little trouble, his name is blessed among researchers. William Buckland was an ambitious man; he was, also, young and impetuous. His name appears twenty-five different times in the heavy old record books of the Richmond County court, still kept in the tiny, two-room Clerk's Office.[8] Five times he was sued for debt, a circumstance which brought no dishonor in that day. A man with no capital was forced to borrow on credit and to depend on his clients for quick payments in order to meet the inevitable obligations for building materials. The eighteenth century ledger will show the delay of years in collecting a debt and in paying off accounts. The merchants of Hobbes' Hole, the nearest mercantile town, were his bankers and his source of supplies. Many of these creditors remain unidentified, but the mercantile house of Ritchie was involved when Buckland decided to settle permanently in this new neighborhood.

Buckland, whose little family had been augmented by the arrival of a baby, rented a house near the Court House for the first three years. Land was hard to come by since it was held in such large extent by two or three families. When a farm of 129 acres, with orchards, houses, etc., known by the unromantic name of Browns, was offered for sale in 1765, Buckland decided to buy it. William Allgood, the owner, had it through his wife's previous marriage but he became so financially involved that he could no longer make payments on the mortgage. Buckland bought it with the written understanding that he would not be held responsible for the mortgage to Archibald Ritchie and placed 225 pounds sterling confidently in the hands of his friend Allgood. It seemed a good bargain, but poor Buckland was ignorant of the law of land-titles and so was shocked to find eighteen months later that Ritchie was foreclosing on his mortgage. In February 1767 the case of Buckland *vs.* Allgood and Ritchie finally came up before the Gentlemen Justices. The court decreed that since "Allgood was not to be found in his Balliwick and not appearing nor any attorney for him the sheriff is to take immediate possession and advertise the same for sale on the first Thursday of January next." Thanks to the slowness of justice, before the sale was advertised Buckland paid off Allgood's debt of eighty pounds and quickly remortgaged Browns to Ritchie for £182 11s. 11d. Buckland paid 305 pounds sterling for the farm but his equity was reduced by this large mortgage. With his house and land he acquired a white servant, a Negro slave, twelve head of cattle, two sheep, thirty hogs, two mares, two boats, books, pewter, corn, tobacco, brandy, cider and featherbeds. He was now a planter as well as a craftsman.[9]

The court records show that during these early years Buckland was employed by the County to construct two public buildings. There are private records, too, which show him to have been the builder of the workhouse. His first recorded payments in the county records are for building the county prison.[10] The fact that this building is called prison and not " gaol " puts it in a different category from other such public edifices. The prisons were larger buildings built for longer confinements. They had separate quarters for men and women and could provide better accommodations for debtors. In 1768 Buckland built the workhouse or poorhouse. We do not know what these two buildings were like, but if they fitted the conventional pattern of the times, they were of brick and two-storied. Robert Wormeley Carter confides to himself in his diary that he " paid Buckland 10,000 lbs. tobo. valued to £100 a very extravagant demand for the workhouse shortly to be finished." [11]

Buckland's other public work consisted of building the glebe house for Lunenburg Parish, his own parish. As all the church records for this period have long ago disappeared we know of this project chiefly through the columns of *The Virginia Gazette*. Under date of July 14, 1767, appeared the following advertisement:

> To be rented and entered upon immediately The new Glebe House of this Parish with all the offices in neat repair. There is a good orchard and a garden new pailed. The whole will be rented with 100 acres of land more or less, etc., by applying to the Rev. Mr. Giberne or Mr. Buckland who will show the premises.

Lunenburg Parish Church, built in 1737, stood northwest of the Court House, and its incumbent after 1762 was the Reverend Isaac William Giberne. This clergyman was one of those strange characters with which the Church of England in America was afflicted. Though his mother was forced to support herself by keeping a lace shop in London, he had received through an uncle, a canon of Lincoln Cathedral, a university education and preference in procuring Virginia parishes. Even his rivals admired his eloquence, and his gambling friends, his luck and charm. After winning the hand of Mary Fauntleroy Beale, a rich widow, he found himself related to all the big-wigs of Richmond County with whom he daily drank and played cards. Colonel Carter felt that the worldly parson was a bad influence for his son but enjoyed his sermons so much that he could not bear to reprove him. Parson Giberne lived on his wife's estate overlooking Rappahannock Creek (now Cat Point). His glebe lands he rented to increase his income. The Bucklands were neighbors, close enough to recognize the dust from his " chariot " as it went down the highway, to and from God and Mammon.[12] The Bucklands were, also, parishioners whom the parson felt called upon to defend even to his patron and friend, the appalling Col. Carter. From Belleville, his seat, on July 8, 1768, the Rev. Mr. Giberne writes;

> I am sorry Buckland should give you cause of complaint I acknowledge I was engaged for him for the plank to you, and some Beef, and I am the more surprised at his Debt to you, as he told me *you* was *his Debtor*. He is, I believe, so much involved and so very negligent of his Affairs, that he keeps but bad accts and is ignorant of the true state of them. However, I shall pay him no more money ' till you are satisfied, especially as ' tis agreable to his own Desires. He is now about a Pidgeon House that was to have been finished the last Fall. When that is done, I shall call for my acct. and give you all the satisfaction in my Power tho I cannot conceive I owe him much as he has had a long time since, a Bill of Exchange, some Tobacco and Linnen etc. . . .
>
> N. B. I find a little note of yours 14 Sept 1767 ' that Buckland had 1000 ft of plank about a fortnight ago, and said I should be answerable for it and that he had had 5 Beeves of you in ye 2 last years and some pickled pork.' Wht could he mean by offering to swear off the plank? [13]

Since the glebe house had been finished the previous year Buckland was either at work on some other parish building under the supervision of Colonel Carter as senior vestryman, or the lumber was simply one of many business deals which the great plantation owners made.

Further proof that the Carter family patronized Mr. Buckland is found in the diaries kept by Robert Wormeley Carter. One entry reads,

> Feb. 6, 1766. Borrowed of my Father 1500 nails to finish my Quarter at Hycory thicket. Buckland this day brought home my Bookcase cost 6-0-0 also put up the Chimney piece of carved work, 2-10-6 in all 8-10-0 also a Plan of a House 1-1-6 in all £9-11-6 this Plan he drew some time agoe.[14]

The writer of this diary was the thwarted son of a dictatorial father. He was forced to continue living at Sabine Hall after his marriage and never to enjoy the independence of his " Hycory Thicket." In spite of managing his father's estate, his own 1,225 acres in Richmond, 1,000 more in Stafford, handling the affairs of the parish and serving one term in the Assembly, time hung heavy on his hands. Not a day passed that he did not win or lose large sums at cards or at some of the neighborhood race tracks. The gambling debts are meticulously preserved in the diary, but the means of paying them always seemed difficult. Cash was a rare commodity, the lack of which increased his dependence on his father, even to the point of pocket-money.

Entries in the diary show that Buckland was kept busy and that he gradually collected a comfortable living. Carter's remarks on his " extravagant " demand for the workhouse shows that he did not undersell himself. Other dealings with the Carters appear:

1769

Sept. 27	Sold to Mr. Buckland 68 lbs beef @2d 11/4	
Oct. 2	paid Crickmore a Servt of Buckland's 4/6 for 2 shutters and rollers. [Probably Venetian blinds]	
21	Sold Buckland a Beef weighing 443 lbs at 2d £ 3-13-11	
	Shoe thread spun by McKaway, weaver, sold to William Buckland 1 lb.[15]	

As the Tayloe daughters married, their father sometimes interested himself in building houses for the brides and grooms. When Rebecca, the second daughter, married Francis Lightfoot Lee, Menokin, a newly built house, was given them by Colonel Tayloe. It is located near Warsaw a little above Mount Airy on the north side of the Rappahannock River, on high land as it drops onto the tidal plain. The central building with hip roof is square, stuccoed, with stone quoins and band courses, two on the front and one on the side façade. It once had symmetrical wings but the kitchen wing has been destroyed. The interior woodwork has a character all its own and presents an architectural puzzle. The stair has square newels and only at upper levels are there easings and ramps of the style of more sophisticated houses of Virginia. In its simple, almost Tudor quality it suggests an earlier date. Perhaps it was a renovation and not an entirely new construction of 1769 but it seems altogether possible that William Buckland worked at Menokin.

Other great houses in the neighborhood of what is now Warsaw probably profited by Buckland's skill, either originally or in their remodeling. One of these, Edgehill, to the south of North Farnham church, overlooks Lancaster Creek and the lowlands towards the river. It was the seat of the Chinn family and was built about 1770.

On the opposite bank of the Rappahannock to the north west of the town of Tappahannock in Essex County lie Blandfield and Elm-

MENOKIN

wood. With Blandfield there is again the Tayloe connection because the Colonel's daughter Jane married Robert Beverley, its owner, in 1760. Beverley was also the nephew of Robert Wormeley Carter. Family notebooks show that the old house was being redecorated and added to between the time of his marriage and 1771.[16] Blandfield is a brick, two-and-a-half-storied house with large rectangular wings connected by an enclosed passageway, rare in Virginia. It bears a distinct resemblance to Annapolis houses, and its plan is almost identical with a plan published in James Gibbs' *Architecture*. Its chief interior distinction is its very spacious hall with two fireplaces. The once beautiful paneling, cornices and mantels fell prey to the eccentricities of wealth in the 1850's.

Elmwood was built soon after the estate was acquired by Muscoe Garnett in 1768 and contains heavily carved woodwork of unusual classical design and beauty. In some ways it has the most monumental and architectural interior woodwork of any house in Virginia. The entablature of the hall is Doric with triglyphs and metopes. Between the entrance hall and the rooms on either side there are semi-circular archways in the thickness of the masonry walls. If this is a design by Buckland, as some think, he had not yet acquired the pleasant domestic scale that he was to employ in his later houses. Among the many houses on both sides of the Rappahannock River these stand out as possible Buckland houses, based entirely on the dates of building and their interior woodwork.

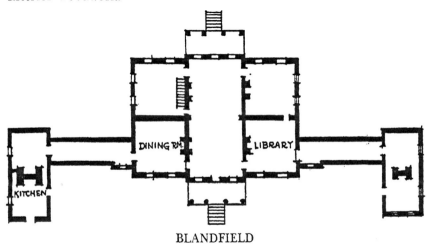

BLANDFIELD

The private life of Mr. Buckland could on occasion be colorful. Once he was presented to the Grand Jury for being a profane swearer, an eighteenth century sin that was not condoned as was drinking and gambling. The fine for this misdemeanor was ten shillings or 100 pounds of tobacco for the use of the poor of Lunenburg Parish.[17] Another time he and a friend were defendants in a case of trespass, assault and battery for which he was held guilty and paid a fine of £ 2 10s. and costs. Only once did he have occasion to employ a lawyer. This worthy, the most prominent attorney in the Northern Neck, Richard Parker, got his neighbor off with a settlement. Twice Buckland had to seek redress through the courts to force a tenant on his farm to pay his rent, and twice he brought in his runaway servants to receive official punishment. He sat on juries; he was a witness for his friends; he surveyed the highway and he inspected the bridges over Totusky Creek. Once he was asked to settle a difference, "his award to be the judgment of the land." [18]

As his reputation grew, so did his work and his family. A wife, two daughters, a son, and two apprentices eventually comprised his immediate household. The system of apprentices in Virginia followed closely that of England. Where the upper classes were largely self-made and dependent on agriculture and trade for their fortunes, it became the universal custom to send the less scholarly sons to neighbors for training. The planters took their young relatives to live with them to teach them plantation management, but taught them, also, a way of life not always consistent with their future means. Other boys were bound out to learn a trade and receive some schooling at the same time. William Buckland, following the custom, took his first apprentice in 1763 and another in 1768. John Randall, the initial pupil, was only thirteen years old and the thirteenth child of a neighboring small planter who had recently died. When his mother remarried and moved to another county, John petitioned the Court to appoint Mr. Buckland his legal guardian, which was granted and recorded on December 1, 1766.[19] Young Randall lived with the Bucklands until William's death, a matter of eleven years. The second apprentice was John Callis, perhaps a son of the man from whom Buckland once bought a silver watch.[20] These two boys were put through the rigid training in joinery and eventually became assets to their instructor.

There was also attached to the family a white maid to care for the children. This Elizabeth White, "a servant wench," was hailed before the Justices for having two bastard children. Only one year later she was given her freedom from indentureship by the sheriff.[21] Apparently the Bucklands had had enough of her kind and thereafter employed only Negroes as household helpers. Oxford, who came with the farm, continued in their service until his master's death, when he was inventoried as William Buckland's most valuable asset. Presumably one of the Negro women, Sue, was Oxford's wife and their two children were also part of the household. Robert Wormeley Carter mentions Crickmore, "Buckland's man servant," coming to Sabine Hall on an errand and Buckland's smith mending a broken lock. Another, a farm hand, James Gilliard, was purchased with the farm and was either sold again with the land, or finished his term of indenture before 1772.

For experienced workmen in joinery or brick-laying Buckland was forced to buy convicts who gave him no end of trouble. The newspapers of the day were largely supported by the paid advertisements of owners of runaway servants. John Ewing, whose name is also spelled Ewen or Ewin, and Samuel Bailey or Bayley, were fugitives on several occasions. They were both joiners, both " remarkably dull and stupid " looking, Bailey being also especially clumsy. In the notices, descriptions of their clothes were always given in great detail for they would have no easy way to secure a change of costume. The reward prescribed by law for their return was forty shillings, but to this "usual reward" masters added extras. In the cases of Ewing and Bailey, Buckland supplemented the reward by another forty shillings. Both men were always found and returned because they never ventured farther than Maryland. The *Gazettes* of both colonies were avidly read in each and they carried many notices from both sides of the Potomac. When the runaways were picked up they were committed to jail temporarily. After their return to their masters they were forced to serve twenty-one extra months following the expiration of their terms of servitude.

The following advertisement in the *Virginia Gazette* (Purdie & Dixon) for August 1, 1771, gives an accurate description of Samuel Bailey:

Runaway from the Subscriber, Last night, a convict servant man named Samuel Bailey, by Trade a House Joiner, and has been in this country about two years. He is a stout wellset Fellow, of a ruddy Complexion, about five feet six or seven inches high, had a foreleg which is much swelled, a Cast with his Eyes, which are large and gray, his Head remarkably Gray, occasioned by the Smallpox, which he is pitted with, his dress is an Osnaburg Shirt, and long Trousers, a light brown Jacket, an old Felt Hatt, old Countrymade shoes tied, and commonly wears a green Worsted Cap. All Masters of Vessels are forewarned from harbouring or employing him. I will give a Reward of Forty shillings to any person who will deliver the said Servant to me, besides what the Law Allows.

William Buckland

Ewing and Bailey eventually gave up their desire to escape, settled down to become two of his best workmen. Their seven years' term, which was the convicts' lot, was not completed at Buckland's death, for both men appear in the inventory of the estate.[22]

One other man also worked in the shop on the highway. His name is unknown because he did not tempt his fate by running away. Perhaps he was, like his master, a serious craftsman. In the only surviving letter from Buckland's pen he mentions, " I have now some of the Best Workmen in Virginia among whom is a London Carver, a masterly Hand." [23]

To what other work did this competent crew turn its hands? It is important to note that Buckland never advertised for work. The notices of his runaway servants and a letter or two for him at the post office are the only evidences of his existence that appeared in the press. He was probably never without commissions. He drew plans, he designed and executed woodwork both carved and plain, he supervised construction and he made furniture. There was evidently a continuing demand by the wealthy planters for one or the other of his talents. Mansions were in constant need of repair or additions, and the generation coming of age was anxious to redecorate " in the modern style." In 1769 Menokin was ready for occupancy, while the work at Blandfield and Elmwood would have just commenced.

Riding up and down the sandy roads of the Northern Neck, the former London apprentice-boy was busy. He was now a man of some means and standing in the community, a man of property, a man who was lifting his profession from the hands of amateurs.

Buckland had been in some difficulty with Councillor Robert Carter of Nomini over a right of way and boundaries. Their lands were adjacent, though Nomini's 2,500 acres lay in the county of Westmoreland. Addressed to the " Honble Robert Carter, Esq." a letter is endorsed as " received 27th March 1771."

Honerd Sr

I have just now heard of your being in these Parts and send of the Bearer with this to Request the Faviour of you to lett me know what day it will be agreable for you for me to wait on you as I flatter myself I should be able to explain the Nature of my Intentions to the Bill of Land in dispute to yr Honrs satisfaction and I have so high an opinion of your Willingness to do justice to all mankind that after having laid my Papers before you I could with great pleasure submit the whole to yr Determination. I am and shall continue to be uneasii while I think I Labour under your Displeasure for I have long hopd for an opertunitie of being im-

ployed (in the way of my Profesion) in some jobb under yr Honr
Should I ever be so Fortunate I think I should aim to aquitt myself
to your satisfaction. I mention this because I have lately heard you
had some notion of making Nomony your sumers Residence I
have now some of the Best Workmen in Virginia among whom is
a London Carver a masterly Hand It is Probable that you will
before you leave these Parts be within sight of my shop Should yr
Fondness for Work of that kind and Drawings induce you to call
in I shall ever Remember the Honr done me The last time you
was up I was so unfortunate as not to know it till it was too late
for you was sett of home the day before I gott to Nomony your
consenting to my Waiting on you will confer a lasting obligation
on Sr

Yr Honrs most obetit. hbl.
sert.

W Buckland
March ye 25th 1771 [24]

While eminently respectful, the writer stands up for himself and
suggests that their legal quarrel might be settled out of court. He also
manages to get in some rather tactful advertising. He knew he was up
against a man learned in the law, a member of the Governor's Council,
and that discretion was the better part of valor. The case was brought
into the June Court of Richmond County and there settled. There is
no way of telling whether Buckland was ever given a chance to work on
the additions to Nomini Hall, made when the Carter family removed
permanently from Williamsburg to their plantation. Their Princeton
tutor, Philip Fithian, spoke of plans for remodeling:

> January 27, 1774 The Colonel is making preparations for a Jour-
> ney to Annapolis, where he Designs next month . . . He and Mrs
> Carter shewed me their House; the original Design, the present
> form; & what is yet to be done.[25]

Did the Councillor go to Annapolis to consult his old neighbor, William
Buckland?

It was only a few months after he wrote Councillor Carter that
Buckland took another decisive step in his life. As we shall see later,
he had been away from his family for weeks at a time as work opened
up to him in Maryland. When in September, 1771, young Edward
Lloyd of Wye sent for him to meet him in Annapolis in order to

discuss the building of a house there, Buckland determined to give up the life of a traveling man and to settle in the busy capital of Maryland.[26] It was a healthier place, not subject to the curse of ague and fevers. Mary and the children would have all the conveniences of city life, and he would profit by a more lucrative practice. He returned from Annapolis, taking the better part of three days to cover one hundred miles, with three ferriages and seventy-nine farm gates to open and close en route.[27] As usual he had no extra money either for a move or for running two establishments. John Randall was to come to Annapolis with him. John Callis could stay at the Virginia shop to see that present work was finished and to be helpful to Mrs. Buckland. The Lloyd woodwork could be done in Virginia as well as anywhere for it would take time to find suitable living quarters and a shop in a comparatively crowded city. He was to draw a good salary and expenses from Lloyd starting December, 1771, but he knew from experience that payments were always slow.

Whereupon Buckland entered upon the approved banking transaction of the times, mortgaged his live-stock and furniture for a six-month period for the sum of £80. Archibald McCall, merchant of Tappahannock, made the loan but never had to possess himself of the Buckland goods and chattels, as the mortgage was paid off promptly in April of 1772.[28] Subsequently the farm was sold and most of the furniture carted aboard a Rappahannock schooner for conveyance to Annapolis. As city folk the Bucklands would no longer need their ox-cart, their chair and harness, and they left behind forever the cattle, sheep and hogs of their farming days. The journey of Mary Buckland, the three children, Mary, Sarah and Francis, the slaves and the four indentured craftsmen, was made during the summer months. The last heard of them in Richmond County was when they failed to answer the summons to court in September to show cause why Elizabeth White, the errant servant wench, should not have her freedom.[29] The Bucklands had gone, bag and baggage; Elizabeth's indenture time was up and so she was free. Her master and mistress had begun a new chapter in their lives.

GUNSTON HALL where Buckland first
worked in America. The garden portico,
overlooking the tidal Potomac, shows the
Gothic pointed arch together with Renaissance details—a combination seen in lower
picture from Batty Langley's pattern book
known to have been in Buckland's library.

Interiors at Gunston where Buckland displayed his skill in joinery in the latest London fashion to gratify his patron's taste. The frilled cornice of the dining room windows shows a Chinese influence new to the Colonies.

The entrance hall at Gunston, showing the door to the
garden (under the landing) , the two elliptical arches,
the pendent pineapple and the elaborate stair rail.

POHICK CHURCH.

Note the Ionic architectural frame for the inscriptions and the decorated cornice around the room.

ROCKLEDGE.

One of the few stone residences on which Buckland worked and one of his first commissions after leaving Gunston.

BLANDFIELD. The spreading plan and the formal symmetry were duplicated many times in English country houses of the 18th century, and illustrated in the plan books in Buckland's library.

MENOKIN. The square newels, rails with but occasional easings, and the four balusters to the tread, all reflect a style of earlier date than that seen in Buckland's more sophisticated houses.

ELMWOOD. The high Renaissance curved and broken pediments and the suppressed frieze of the doorways are in an entirely different spirit. The mantel is a later addition.

54

Copy of James Stoddert's map of Annapolis, made for
John Ridout, showing the State House Circle, Church
Circle, Bloomsbury Square where Buckland lived, the
docks and the harbor.

UPTON SCOTT HOUSE. The street front shows the all-header bond of the brickwork, the slight projection of the three central bays under the pediment, the bracketed cornice, and the fine entrance.

The entrance hall of the Scott house, widened to accommodate the beautifully decorated stair. The archway affords access to the garden.

The garden side of the RIDOUT HOUSE. The Palladian window interrupts the main cornice. Tall chimneys and the high portico give great dignity.

The mantel and wall panels of the Ridout dining room, with detail of painted panel let into the decorated frieze.

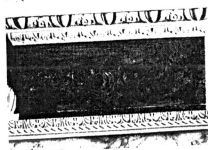

Portico at WHITEHALL before the architectural decoration
of the entrance was installed in 1957. The most monumental
of all designs which have been attributed to Buckland.

The bay side of Whitehall after alterations of 1957.

The land side of Whitehall after alterations.

Whitehall. Carved wood mask decoration above the cornice in tray ceiling of the great hall.

Interior of the entrance doorway, attribute to Buckland, one of the few instance known of his use of the Corinthian orde The scroll bracket terminating the windo trim was one of Buckland's favorite motif

Maison de Campagne, près d'Annapolis, E.U.

Watercolor of STRAWBERRY HILL made
by a French officer visiting Annapolis in 1797.

TULIP HILL. The graceful portico, the suppressed
pediment and sculptured details add charm to the design.

Tulip Hill. Segmental arches and
pendent rose before elaborate stair.

Cupid of the portico.

"G" for Galloway over
bull's-eye window.

MONTPELIER. The garden front, showing the steep pediment and roof, and the semi-octagonal bays to the wings – fairly usual features surviving from Tudor times.

The turned balusters, three to the tread, and painted wainscot with mahogany cap are notable.

Corner cupboard and mantel at Montpelier showing Corinthian pilasters with undercut capitals, the decorated
cornice with its convex frieze much used by Buckland.

Maryland

THE JOURNEY up from Virginia was a familiar one to William Buckland. He had before this time interviewed prospective builders, "waited on Gentlemen," presented designs and sometimes accompanied his craftsmen when they installed a chimney-piece or paneled room. It was not difficult to put horse and carved work aboard a schooner docking at Totusky Creek on the Rappahannock. With a fair wind one could expect to arrive in Annapolis harbor some three days later.

In the decade before Buckland made Annapolis his home, his contribution to the architecture of Maryland was considerable, because of frequent visits. What was this new center of his activities like? The town in which he was to leave so many proofs of his artistry was more approachable by water than by land. A peninsula scalloped by creeks from bay and river, it could be reached by highway only from the west where the road meandered around the upper reaches of the Patuxent River from the crossroads of Upper Marlboro, a gateway to the south. The well-sheltered harbor, however, gave berth to ships from Bristol, London, Glasgow, Cork, the West Indies and all coastal ports. Barges and snows plied the bay's estuaries, bringing local tobacco, farm produce, bricks and lumber to this, one of the chief markets in the colonies.[1] Only from the perspective of Greenberry Point could the one hundred year old town be seen in its full size and beauty. From this point in the outer harbor, the tall chimneys, the square tower of St. Anne's Church, and the giant trees made background for the shoreline of docks and terraced lawns.

Annapolis had been laid out in 1694 by a cultivated professional governor. Whether Sir Francis Nicholson was the first practitioner of zoning in the colonies is a moot question, but it is certain that he planned his new capital with all due care for attractiveness and business.[2] On the highest hill he placed the official buildings. From this eminence, looking down the radiating streets, could be seen the two approaches to the city, the blue waters of the harbor, and, in the opposite direction, the city gates. Since he governed by royal decree in a lapse of Lord Baltimore's control, the Established Church was seated in another circle, only a little smaller and a little lower than that occupied by the capitol building. Industry and trade were restricted to one part of the town, gentlemen's estates to the bank of the river, and tradesmen's homes to a defined square.[3] The streets were named for members of the royal family or after those in London. Unfortunately, Sir Francis departed before all his civic planning had been brought to completion.

In the seventy-five years that followed, Annapolis grew in an orderly fashion. The salaries of Lord Baltimore's public servants grew fatter with the increase of business or by collections of quit rents and endless fees; inhabitants multiplied and the census in 1768 stood at 1,200. The population was made up of prosperous tobacco merchants, government officials and a laboring class. The city had early taken on a look of permanency with its brick government buildings and dwellings, though the Golden Age of its architecture was still a few years off.

Under the influence of Governor Robert Eden and his wife, the sister of Frederick Calvert, 6th Lord Baltimore, the moneyed class aped the gaiety of London. The preceding governor, Colonel Horatio Sharpe, was a bachelor and an old warrior, more interested in relaxing from official duties at his plantation than in participating in an active social life. Not so the Edens, who led a Court Circle into all the extravagances of the times. Visitors remarked on the pleasure loving life in their letters home. "An universal Mirth and Glee reigns . . . amongst all Ranks of People and at set times, nothing but Jollity and Feasting goes forward." "The object of the Inhabitants here is altogether pleasure. Business is no part of their system." [4]

Business had, however, provided the wealth of the colonists. Tobacco went out of the harbor, cheap labor and luxury goods of every kind came in. The class distinctions of the old country fell before rising fortunes. With no loss of dignity could a member of the Governor's Council compete in exports and imports with a man who had, perhaps, arrived as an indentured servant only a few years earlier. Nor was there great distinction between wholesale and retail business when a merchant lived next to his warehouse or shop and advertised a mixed cargo in the weekly press. The Governor's brother captained his own ship, *The Annapolis*, in the tobacco trade and the fastidious Colonel Fitzhugh ran what would now be called a bakery to supply ships with loaf bread.[5] One merchant dealt entirely in leather, another in bricks made of good Anne Arundel clay, another in lumber or in wool, but all speculated in land and all met at the Assembly Rooms for an evening of dancing. It was a society based almost entirely on wealth.

Building town houses had been given impetus by the arrival of the Edens in 1768. To be sure, Annapolis was surrounded by comfortable country seats, Primrose Hill, Acton, Belvoir, Stepney and Whitehall, but planters who lived farther afield decided it was high time to have city houses when they came to town for business or court.[6] More often their wives decided it for them.

Although there were already established in Annapolis several men capable of drawing plans for houses, they did it chiefly as an avocation. Mr. William Noke, was collector of Lord Baltimore's quit rents; Mr. Charles Wallace, senior partner of the largest mercantile house in town. To the latter was given the contract for erecting the new "Stadt House." This commission drew forth from a friend in the *Homony Club*, a social organization, the following laudatory verses:

> By different methods, different men excell
> If Paca speaks, yet Wallace acts as well,
> Intent this Town and country to befriend,
> and fond to useful works his hand to lend,
> He rears the Column and projects the Dome,
> and makes our streets like those of ancient Rome.
> A grateful People shall preserve thy Fame;
> and rank with Jones and Wren thy honored name.
> But tho the Trav'ler views with pleased Surprise
> Stupendous Fabricks reaching to the Skies,
> Admires the Structures and applauds thy Art,
> 'Tis mine to praise the Goodness of thy Heart,
> Thy many social Virtues to commend,
> The useful Citizen and Public Friend.[7]

Wallace was indeed the "useful citizen" but would have laughed at posterity trying to credit him with being an architect. Two men there were, however, who had had some English training. Robert Key, an English friend of the Governor's, was entrusted with enlarging and redecorating the Jenings' mansion for the gubernatorial palace. He had also designed the new theatre, complete with boxes, pit and gallery, and was ready to start on the new church whenever the Governor gave the word.[8] Joseph Horatio Anderson called himself an architect as well as a planter. In a recently discovered letter of 1770 he states that he is designing the State House at Annapolis.[9] This verifies the tradition that a man named Anderson was the architect. These men were capable of designing and erecting the many buildings planned for the town, but in 1771 when Buckland arrived, all were busily engaged. None of them had as much training and talent as Buckland.

There are a number of houses, both in Virginia and Maryland, with which the name of William Buckland has been associated, but Annapolis is the seat of most of his surviving work. It is important in evaluating his achievements to recognize that in most cases the shell of the house was completed by the time his services were required, so that the preponderance of his work is joinery. The houses are almost without exception of brick, four-square, with hip roofs, white cornice and tall chimneys that give great distinction to the imposing mass. They reflect the economic well-being of the colony. Along the seaboard the dangerous and uncertain conditions of frontier life were past, and no longer satisfied with the simple houses of their fathers and grandfathers, the builders sought to express in their homes the prominence they enjoyed in the community.

The interiors imitated the elegance and refinement of the London houses of the gentry. Many in this wave of confidence and prosperity turned to Buckland as the one best qualified to fulfill their desires, and the interiors of these attributed houses might well be the creation of one mind, for the motives repeat again and again. The three elements of the classical entablature are used with skill and assurance, and seldom is there any deviation from accepted formulae illustrated in the pattern books and learned by Buckland during his apprentice days in London. The architrave is bent to serve as trim around door and window. The frieze, usually decorated, occurs over door and window and in the mantel. The decorated cornice, either straight or in broken pediment where accent is required, is placed over doorways and mantels and around the rooms. Although there is little documentary evidence in most cases to prove the authorship of the elegant detail in these houses there is a resemblance in the craftmanship.

In a sparsely settled community all the gentry were on more or less intimate terms, if not actually blood-relations. Northern Virginia and Southern Maryland were as one colony. Marriages between families were frequent. We have seen this Maryland-Virginia intermarriage in the Mason family and it was, also, an ordinary occurrence in the Tayloe, Carter, Lee, Fitzhugh and Brent families. These great clans had the same standards of living and social interests. What was more natural than their sharing information on the merits or demerits of house builders? Building a house was an important event in any colonist's life but with those who had been educated in England and knew the scale of the ordinary country-gentleman's seat, or even aspired to emulate the nobility, it became a matter of the deepest concern.

A contemporaneous account of Annapolis gives a vivid picture of the architectural awakening there in 1769:

> The buildings in Annapolis were formerly of small dimensions, and of an inelegant construction; but there are now several modern edifices which make a good appearance. There are few habitations without gardens; some of which are planted in a decent stile, and are well stocked. At present, this city has more the appearance of an agreeable village, than the metropolis of an opulent province, as it contains within its limits a number of small fields which are intended for future erections. But in a few years, it will probably be one of the best built cities in America, as a spirit of improvement is predominant, and the situation is allowed to be equally healthy and pleasant with any on this side of the Atlantic . . . It is the seat of Government; the public offices are here established; and as many of the principal families have chosen this place for their residence, there are few towns of the same size in any part of the British dominions, that can boast a more polished society . . . In the vicinity are many pleasant villas, whose proprietors are eminent for their hospitality.[10]

Around the year 1765 seven great Maryland houses were being built, all of which show the Buckland influence. These are Dr. Upton

Scott's and John Ridout's Annapolis residences; Richard Sprigg's Strawberry Hill and Horatio Sharpe's Whitehall, both on the outskirts of Annapolis; Galloway's Tulip Hill farther out in Anne Arundel County; the Snowdens' Montpelier in Prince George's County, and the Ringgold house in Chestertown. All but Strawberry Hill were of brick, and all but that mansion are still standing. All were adorned with the elaborate woodwork which was Buckland's forte.[11]

Dr. Scott, John Ridout and Governor Sharpe would have employed the same man to do the designs for their houses, if it were possible, for they were intimate friends with similar tastes. Sharpe and Scott had fought together in the British forces where the Governor was a career colonel and Upton Scott an army surgeon. When William Sharpe, one of young Lord Baltimore's guardians, had procured the governorship for his brother, Upton Scott had come along to Maryland as his personal physician. Dr. Scott further intrenched his own interests by marrying Elizabeth Ross, a daughter of Lord Baltimore's Secretary of the Council, Collector of his Lordship's quit-rents and Register of the Land Office. As time went on Scott inherited these same sinecures from John Ross, his father-in-law, so that with his large medical practice the poor Belfast doctor was able to plan for himself the finest of town houses. Daniel Dulany writing to Councilor Robert Carter so esteemed it: " Dr Scott has built the best Town House in America." A year later a mob of country people came to town to intimidate the Council and took it out in " menaces against the best building viz Dr. Scot's house." [12] In a letter written a few days after this affair, Scott goes into more detail:

> The whole continent of America is at present in the utmost confusion on account of an act of Parliament made last year imposing a Stamp Duty upon them. God knows what the events will be if the Government should insist on its being carried into execution. I shall be involved in the commotion which most probably will attend this Country in the struggle.
>
> I am at present exceedingly hampered on acct. of the expense of building a house which is not yet finished, my workmen having persued measures that have run away with more cash than I proposed. Some political Storms, which I have not yet entirely weathered, had lately, very nearly swallowed me up.[13]

These letters with a 1762 advertisement by the good doctor for a brick-maker " who understands his business," definitely date the building. Once set in extensive gardens with a colonial rarity, a greenhouse, the house still overlooks its erstwhile terraces to the nearby creek. The Scott house is of brick, all header bond on the long sides, a simple rectangle in plan. The symmetrical and detached outbuildings are of later date. A shallow projection surmounted by a pediment, reminiscent of Blandfield, gives variety to the entrance façade. The entrance doorway is pedimented over a Doric order with triglyphs. The garden side has a high and narrow Doric portico very like the broader one on the Ridout house. The main cornice is supported by uncommon brackets that extend into the frieze above a suppressed architrave. Tall chimneys add distinction to its imposing effect. Of the interior woodwork little survives but that on the first floor and in the beautifully proportioned doorways. Dr. Scott returned from a self-inflicted exile during the Revolution to find that his popularity was in no way impaired, so beloved was he by the citizenry of Annapolis. Here and at his wife's plantation, Belvoir, he continued to a ripe old age to grow rare plants and enjoy his garden.

The second of the trio of intimate friends was John Ridout. He also arrived in Maryland with Governor Sharpe. A graduate of Oxford, he served as personal secretary to the Governor, rising to high office in the government. He was credited with being the brains of the administration. When in 1765 Mary Ogle, the daughter of a former governor and the sister of a future one, had to choose between two suitors for her hand, she picked the young secretary rather than the middle-aged Sharpe. Ridout then built on his lot on Duke of Gloucester Street, and here within waving distance of Dr. Scott on the one hand and their Dulany relations on the other, they passed the remainder of their days. This impressive house with its free-standing wings and garden terraced to the harbor, has a commanding exterior and a simpler interior than other contemporary houses. It is of brick laid all headers. There is the usual central block. The dependencies exist as separate entities but appear as in the Scott house, to have been built later than the main house. The architectural elaboration is restrained. At the entrance there is a pediment over two engaged columns. The rear entrance, overlooking the garden and the harbor, has a Doric porch with high stoop. Above it, a Palladian window, centrally located on the second floor, is allowed to interrupt the main cornice in order to obtain the necessary height for the semi-circular sash. It is a problem that is always difficult and not too well handled here. Though the chimney pieces and woodwork are not as elaborate as in documented Buckland houses the drawing room's lacy plaster cornice is unusually fine.

Much has been written about the man who brought both Scott and Ridout to Annapolis. Suffice it to say that he was primarily a military man, one time commander-in-chief of His Majesty's forces defending Virginia and the neighboring colonies from the French and Indians; a bachelor and an excellent governor. Like all soldiers, he dreamed of a home of his own. Since there was no official residence for the governor, Sharpe was forced to rent a suitable town house. Ten years after his arrival he was able to bring his dreams to fruition by purchasing a large tract of land at the mouth of the Severn River, on the opposite shore from Annapolis. Here he built what one visitor called " a box of a house." This eventually became the central unit of a mansion built on a grand scale. An overall length of 258 feet was planned, but the extremities, to include running-water bathrooms, were apparently never constructed. Building continued, however, up to the time of the unexpected request from Lord Baltimore that he retire from his official position in favor of Caroline Calvert's young husband, Captain Robert Eden. Shocking as this news must have been to a conscientious and popular governor, Sharpe, nevertheless, took it philosophically. Farming appealed to him, he felt the Maryland climate beneficial and the Annapolitans his friends. He wrote to England, " I shall be happy in cultivating my Garden." But in 1773, his house still uncompleted in some details, he returned to visit his brothers and was caught in England by the Revolution. Like most Britishers who had taken an oath to support the king, he felt that he could not again become a Marylander. But twenty years in the colonies and memories of his beloved Whitehall kept him ever in touch with the Ridout family in whose care he had left his estate. At his death in 1790, Whitehall, which had escaped confiscation through the efforts of Ridout and his Ogle brother-in-law, became legally Ridout property. For over one hundred years it remained the family's summer residence.[14]

Whitehall was at first one story without wings. At a later date the second story was added and the wings extended, which achieved in total a most imposing and pleasing effect. The portico overlooking the broad waters of the Bay is the most monumental feature known on any Maryland colonial residence. It is one of the earliest examples of the classical colonnade.

One enters directly into a square hall extending entirely through the house. Its tray ceiling reaches up into the roof. To each side is a square room. That is the original and central plan. At the time that the second story was added a small stair hall was built at each side to lead to the bedroom above. The upper part of the hall separates these two rooms which had no communication except through the hall

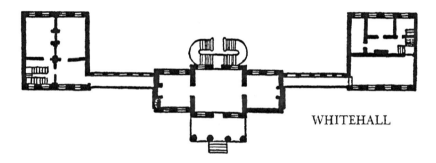

WHITEHALL

below. The window trim in the hall ends in a beautifully decorated scroll above the level of the sill, in a manner very similar to that at the Hammond house, and in the dining room and sitting room opposite, the trim is elaborated in a great flair. The mantel in the dining room is quite elaborate with eggs and darts, dentils and acanthus leaves.

Just what part Buckland had in the execution of Whitehall is uncertain. The present owner has done considerable research on the subject and owns unsigned plans. He feels that while another than Buckland may have drawn these, the latter was responsible for carrying out the joinery. Most assuredly the interiors show great competence and familiarity with the best Georgian precedent and are not unlike the work done by Buckland in other Annapolis houses. The strongest motive for crediting him with the woodwork of Whitehall is the fact that no other man of the period capable of executing the design is known. Governor Sharpe visited and hunted with George Mason at Gunston, so it is likely that he was acquainted with Buckland. And the intimate ties of friendship which bound Sharpe, Ridout and Scott make it reasonable to believe that Buckland was commissioned to work on the houses of all three.

A handsome country seat near Annapolis rising from a hilly peninsular across Dorsey's Creek, with an expansive view out to the Bay, was built about 1766. Charles Willson Peale was an intimate of the owner of Strawberry Hill, had tea often with him and went " walking with his gun " to shoot birds on the 600-acre estate. In his autobiography Peale associates Buckland with the house when he writes " This farm possesses some beautiful views and the buildings, especially the Mansion-house, is in fine taste of architecture designed by Mr. Buckley for Mr. Spriggs a wealthy friend." [15] Mr. Peale was a notoriously bad speller in an era when there was little conformity on that subject, and his active mind, forgetful of facts during fifty intervening years, was on many things as he jotted down his notes. He was, however, not only a friend of the owner of Strawberry Hill but also a friend of William Buckland. Since the name Buckley is unknown in those parts it may safely be assumed that " Buckley " was intended for Buckland.

When Richard Sprigg of Cedar Park, West River, married Margaret Caile, the family tradition is that his Quaker mother urged him to leave the dull country-side and take his bride to the gayer city scene. It was then, in 1766, that he bought 60 acres of undeveloped land patented as Dorsey, built his house and laid out orchards and gardens that made the place famous. Friends remarked on the extravagance of the outlay. " I join you in an opinion that R. Sprigg, Esqr. has paid for that little plantation though I suppose it was to please, for I am rong if she don't like great company as they call it there." [16]

The only picture of Strawberry Hill extant is a small watercolor, made in 1797 by a visiting French officer, showing its commanding position and its portico. The house was frame with two two-story wings, gable roof with chimney at each end and the owner was one of the highest taxpayers in the county.[17] Here in the fall of 1773 Colonel George Washington was entertained at dinner before the theatre.[18] At this time he would have met four of the five little girls born to his host and hostess. He would, also, have attended the Annapolis race meet as the special guest of the steward of the Jockey Club, Richard Sprigg.

A little farther from the bustle of Annapolis lived another Quaker, a neighbor and cousin of Richard Sprigg, also born and bred on West

River. He was, however, never truly indoctrinated with the Quaker desire for a simple life. It is said that he changed his church in order to get his wife, and for her, too, he built a beautiful house with many romantic details. Samuel Galloway was an enterprising merchant-planter, who built a fleet of schooners and snows at his own yards, carried tobacco from the Southern Maryland counties to England and brought back not only goods but also large numbers of indentured servants. His warehouses and docks lined the shore of West River and there, as well as in the city marts, he sold off his cargoes. With the expansion of his family and his fortune, Galloway picked a pretty site for a new house for his invalid wife. Anne Chew Galloway, unfortun-

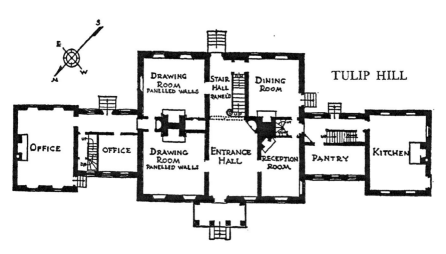

TULIP HILL

ately, did not live to see the mansion completed, for she died in December of 1756. Galloway continued building, adding wings, handsome mantels faced with imported marble, and delicately carved woodwork. He became one of the greatest horse breeders in the colonies, the owner of the imported Othello, sire of his Selim, the fastest race-horse of his day.[19] Galloway was a friend of Colonel Washington who frequently stopped for dinner at Tulip Hill on his way to or from Annapolis.[20] Farming and horses they had in common but not politics, for Galloway was but a lukewarm patriot. The secret stair, walled within one of the great double chimneys, was perhaps a quick escape to the lawn and the boat landing should neighborhood patriotism grow too hot. But undisturbed, the place continued in the family for one hundred years.

One can be reasonably sure that Buckland's connection was very like that with other houses built at an earlier period. The Galloways called upon him towards the end of the construction period, after the main fabric of the house was completed, for which bricks were ordered as early as 1756. Not until 1763 were marble facings ordered from Cork in Ireland, at which date it can be assumed that the house was ready for interior finish. The wings were not added until 1787, long after Buckland's death.[21]

The interior woodwork is much simpler than that at Gunston. The division between the stair hall and the widened entrance hall is marked by two segmental arches joined by an unusual foliated pendentive similar to that at Gunston. The fine corner cupboard contains a carved shell ornament. One may hazard a guess that Buckland was responsible for the entrance portico and the cantilevered canopy with gay frill over the south entrance. It is noteworthy that he never repeated the Chinese details of his first commission. Although most of his houses have a very simple straight baluster, the stair at Tulip Hill has turned balusters. While there is no documentary proof, there are many evidences that it is the work of the same hand that fashioned the woodwork of Gunston Hall and of the Hammond house.

Twenty-five miles southwest of Annapolis in Prince George's County, lies the several thousand acre Snowden estate. Built about 1720 by " the ironmaster," Richard Snowden, Montpelier was enlarged and redecorated by his son, Thomas, after he came into possession of the property in 1770. The additions and the changes in style are clearly discernible where two types of brick bond were used and two types of paneling. Again it can be assumed that Buckland was employed to supply the interior finish. Here he indulged his love and talent for detail to a much greater extent than at Tulip Hill. The stair hall is widened to take the first run of stairs to a landing that extends over the front door. This allows an unobstructed view in both directions and avoids the more usual interference of stair. The stair is more elaborate than we have come to expect of Buckland. The balusters, three to the tread, are turned and the newels and easings are gracefully contrived. The spandril is wood paneled. The division between the stair hall and the hall on the garden side is marked by a simple beam supported at each end by fluted pilasters. The mantels, cornices, and chair rails are almost as elaborate as those at Gunston. A corner cupboard in the east drawing room has fluted Corinthian pilasters with undercut volutes. Major Thomas Snowden, with a large acquaintance in Virginia, could readily have heard of Buckland's work and have commissioned him to modernize the old house. Here are the half octagon wings and a dining room with all the charm and finesse which only Buckland could have produced. Since no Snowden papers can be found, Buckland's part in this lovely old place must remain mere surmise.

It would seem a long guess to bring William Buckland to Maryland's Eastern Shore, but in the case of the Ringgold house in Chestertown no guessing is needed. Thomas Ringgold, merchant, bought two houses and joined them with a third in 1767 and mentions in his will of 1772 that his son, another Thomas, was then living in this structure.[22] The son, also a merchant, owner of many cargo ships, married Polly Galloway of Tulip Hill, and did not long survive his father. The Ringgold fortune was even greater than that of the Galloways because the Ringgolds dominated the port of Chestertown, chief port of entry for the upper Eastern Shore. This town was second only to Annapolis in wealth and fashion and was the seat of a customs house. Tobacco was giving way to wheat, both good crops for exportation. The returning ships were crowded to the gunwales with a cash cargo, convict servants. The Ringgolds were principal agents in this country for the firm of Sedgely, Hilhouse and Randolph of Bristol, whose business it was to deport criminals from England.[23] However unsavory this business was, it took on the patina of public service, service to the British government, and to the labor-hungry planters.

The Ringgolds found no other lot in town so convenient to the waterfront and determined to reconstruct the old houses into something in keeping with their means. Thomas, Jr.'s father-in-law, Samuel Galloway, on the other shore of the Bay, undoubtedly recommended Buckland. There is also the likelihood that the elder Thomas knew George Mason. In 1765 he had been a delegate to the General Congress, called to devise means for carrying on the French and Indian War, and his intimacy with the Virginia delegates continued. Two adjacent buildings were to be connected by a new structure. The earlier one built by Nathaniel Palmer he used as the kitchen wing, and the front section, built by Nathaniel Hynson, Jr., gave him access to the Customs House and a water view.[24] From the white portico he could follow his *Swallow*

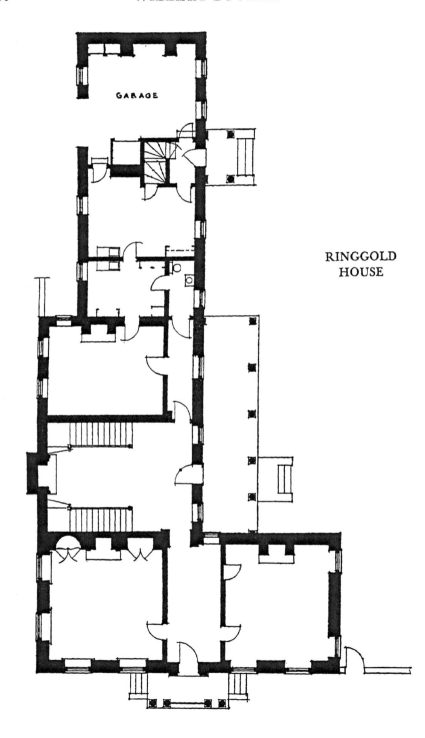

GARAGE

RINGGOLD
HOUSE

and ships of the fleet approaching their anchorage, almost at the garden seawall. In this three-part house he wanted the latest style in woodwork. Here in the central block is a beautiful divided stairway and the rooms are enriched with paneling and elaborately carved chimney pieces. When the paneling in the front section of the house was removed to be installed in the Baltimore Museum of Art it was observed that the design of the paneling did not agree with the original window openings, now closed, in the brick wall revealed by the removal of the woodwork. On the back of this woodwork was discovered the cypher, " WB 1771." [25] It would thus seem that at the time the junction of the three sections was effected, Ringgold installed paneling in the front section that he had purchased. As in some other houses in which Buckland's interiors were installed, the structure of the house was completed before he started his work.

The paneling and the carved decorations of the drawing room are marked by extreme delicacy and refinement. A fret dentil course is placed in all cornices but otherwise the graceful details are confined to overdoors and over-mantels. The chair rails and baseboards, differing from Buckland's interiors in Annapolis, are without carving. On each side of the broken pediment over the mantel are vertical floral designs in the manner of Grinling Gibbons. The marble of the fireplace facing is grey and white, much used at the time. In an effort to adapt the room to modern usage the mantel shelf has been widened by the addition of a top moulding, consisting of fascia and cyma. It has no part in the classical profile of the mantel mould and crowds unpleasantly the over panel. It is a damage frequently met with in old and altered rooms. The stair is a conspicuous feature of the house. It is found in that portion of the complex that joins the two early sections. Two separate flights unite at a landing and continue to the second floor in a single flight. This is the reverse of the double stair in the Chase-Lloyd house. The details of rail, balusters and tread ends may have been designed by Buckland when he installed the woodwork of the parlor and other rooms on the first floor. Occurring as they do in the third and last built portion of the completed house, it is entirely likely.

The history and workmanship of all these Maryland houses built in the years between 1765 and 1772, when Buckland was still a resident of Virginia, indicate that he contributed to their design and had a part in their execution.

VI

Buckland's Annapolis

THE SEPTEMBER day that William Buckland received his summons to meet Edward Lloyd, Esq., in Annapolis was one of the fall racing days. If he had come by boat it was but a step beyond the dock to Middleton's, the best kept inn in town, or to the Ship's Tavern, kept by the widow Marriott. There were ten other hostelries almost as good, but he had put up before at The Crown and Dial, kept by William Faris, and he probably did so again.[1] The loquacious Faris combined tavern keeping with his chosen profession of silver-smithing and clockmaking. The Farises always made a stranger feel welcome for there was a homelike quality to this West Street house with its large family, hospitably inclined towards the more talented artisans of the city. Here could be heard the gossip and chatter of the neighborhood as well as of politics and trade. For eight pence one could have a bed with reasonable assurance that it would not be shared by bedbugs, and for one shilling, six pence, a good hot dinner with a pint of beer.[2]

Bright and early the next morning Buckland sought out his patron at the more luxurious Coffee House. Edward Lloyd was in town to settle his father's estate, attend the races, and execute deeds completing the purchase of Samuel Chase's unfinished house. Lloyd had recently been elected to the Assembly to represent Talbot County and had recently, also, come into a vast fortune.[3] At the gentle prodding of his wife he had agreed that a house of their own in the capital city would be necessary if they were not to run the risk of finding none to rent. Mrs. Lloyd, born Elizabeth Tayloe of Mount Airy, Virginia, had spent her four years of marriage on the Wye plantation, where the first of her seven children had been born, but like most country-bred women she craved a taste of city life.

The house the Lloyds were buying had been half-built by a turbulent young Annapolitan with more ambition and imagination than legal practice. However, his influence with the more radical patriots was increasing daily and the name of Sam Chase was destined to be known throughout the thirteen colonies. In 1769 Chase had purchased a lot on North-East Street, imported a supervising builder from England, and then found that the cost of his dream-house far exceeded his expectation. Lloyd got wind of Chase's desire to sell and for about £3,000 Maryland currency became the owner of four brick walls and a cellar, built in a perfect square.[4] He wanted a plan, other than Chase's, for its completion. When he cast his eye around for the right man to do this, his wife may have suggested a neighbor in Richmond County, Virginia, who had worked for her father, built houses for her sisters and was at the moment under contract to Mr. Ringgold of Chestertown. Thus, in late September, 1771, Buckland came to look over a job that was to keep him almost completely occupied for the next twelve months. It was to be the decisive factor in his removal from Virginia.

Colonel Lloyd wished the grandest house in Annapolis. Another lot must be bought for garden and stables. The house must have full three floors, unusual in Annapolis, with an unobstructed view over the bay to Lloyd's own Eastern Shore. All materials were to be of the best quality and all woodwork was to be handsome without ostentation. Imported marble mantels, solid silver door latches and escutcheons on mahogany doors were regarded as good taste for those who could afford them. Buckland agreed to carry out Lloyd's plans, and he further agreed to begin work in two months' time.[5]

Having satisfactorily settled this business, William Buckland took time off to relax and look around before his trip home. Here was opportunity for the fulfillment of his ambition. The scene he surveyed offered possibilities in his profession unobtainable in the rural districts of Virginia. Building materials were available from a dozen merchant-specialists as well as from the general importers. The wealth of the whole colony of Maryland was drawn to Annapolis and one had but to tap it. There were signs of it in all directions—in the luxurious shops of Church Street where everything from wigs to shoe-buckles could be found; on West Street where coachmakers were inscribing heraldic designs on the high gloss of coach doors and at the docks where white sails were being spread for the outward voyage. Thirty silversmiths and lapidarians tempted the full skirted ladies who were, perhaps, merely visiting the mantua maker next door. Black, liveried coachmen were readying their horses to take their masters and mistresses out to the race grounds. Sailors walked arm in arm with pretty country girls. Peddlers from as far away as Connecticut trudged with their wares. Stout citizens in satin waistcoats passed along the narrow streets. A halfgrown boy, between beats on a drum, was calling out the bargains to be had at a vendue before the first race, " To be sold, the effects of the late Honorable Edward Lloyd, Esq. of ' Wye.' Come ye! Come ye! " [6]

As he made his way up Francis Street to the hill on which stood the public buildings, Buckland could see that the demolition of the old State House was under way. On the public green his attention was attracted to two citizens who would not attend today's race, probably the only two! There stood for all to see a noisy townsman sobering up at the pillory. Nearby the last convicted thief hung on the gibbet. It was but a step from the State House hill to the circle of paling surrounding St. Anne's Church, old and shabby, and remarked on by every visitor as far gone in decay.[7]

Out West Street, Buckland followed the crowd, walking the half mile of muddy road beyond the city gates to the race grounds. Here the Lloyd auction was set up in a booth where free toddy was offered along with a wide collection from a gentleman's household goods. Buckland bought " sundries," but what they were we do not know. For seven pounds he could have had one of the chafing dishes, books, or all sorts of finery, though much of the latter was announced as " Rat eaten." [8] The Virginia countryside rarely offered him such bargains. As the sale drew to an end the first races were announced. Booths for drinks and baubles were near the entrance to the grounds and the surrounding fields were crowded with tethered horses, chaises, every variety of cart and carriage. Over two thousand spectators were on hand. There in the paddock could be seen the gentlemen of the Jockey Club. Here were the ladies, powdered and gay, seated in the family " chariots " to get a better view and surrounded by their swains. On a platform in the center of the circular track were the Governor and distinguished guests. Among them appeared the tall form of a fellow Virginian, Colonel George Washington, and with him was a youth dressed like a peacock, his stepson, " Mr. Custis." [9]

Buckland must put a few shillings on Colonel Lloyd's mare for auld lang syne as he had followed her career since the time she had been owned by Colonel Tayloe in Richmond County. The odds on Nancy Bywell were good and to his immense pleasure, the mare showed her fleet heels to the favorite.[10] This piece of good fortune gave him a little more spending money. Perhaps he would take in the play that evening, a double header, " The Roman Father " followed by the popular " Mayor of Garret." [11]

The next day saw Mr. Buckland on his way home to Virginia. Before he could move his household to Annapolis, there was still work to be finished at his Richmond County shop. The Lloyd interiors must be started, Menokin was not yet completed and his friend, Bernard Sears, was sounding him out about carved work for the new Pohick Church.

The carefully preserved papers of the Lloyd family contain itemized accounts with Chase at the time of transfer of the property and the progress of construction under Lloyd until completion.[12] There is probably no house of colonial America whose construction is so completely documented, and a careful study of the accounts throws light upon the building methods of the time, the different stages of construction under Lloyd, and the actual work done by various craftsmen.

These accounts placed Buckland in Annapolis and at work supervising the construction of the house on December 22, 1771. We know that he brought John Randall with him at that time. Since this former apprentice and ward was now of age, he was his chief assistant.[13] Although construction was well advanced when Buckland had his first conference with Edward Lloyd, it is probable that the brick work around the important exterior features had been delayed, since designs and details for the main entrance and the Palladian window required the skill of an experienced joiner. From October 12 to November 2, 1772, Buckland was reimbursed in the sum of £33:5:0. for workmen's wages and for lime, wood, sheet lead, 2,800 bricks, hair, sundries and " 2 screw plates." We conclude that during these two weeks he was engaged in the design and execution of the main entrance doorway and the Palladian window for which these enumerated materials would have been required; the bricks for the arch over the window, the screw plates for the ends of a tie rod to take the thrust of the arch, and the sheet lead for the flashing.

There is an existing tradition that the house was originally planned by Chase as a two-story house and that Lloyd was responsible for the addition of the third floor. If true, this would explain items on other Buckland accounts in the Lloyd ledgers, now difficult to understand, such as the repeated order for shingles.

Buckland worked intermittently on the Chase-Lloyd house during 1772, after which time another "undertaker," William Noke, seems to have been in charge. Lloyd paid Noke wages from November 2, 1772, to October of 1774, and £370 for materials and labor. The unusually large sum of £900 for "carpenters and joiners" suggests that the stair construction and the interior trim of the upper floors might have been involved. However, by this time Lloyd had added lot #90 to his property on which a large stable and coach house was in process of construction and it would seem more likely that this was the scene of Noke's labors. During 1774, after Buckland had left the job, Noke was building "the party wall" between the property of Lloyd and that of Benjamin Ogle. The cost, £380, was borne equally by both owners.

The decorative plaster work of the house interior was done by Rawlings & Barnes, acting as subcontractors for Noke. They advertised in the *Maryland Gazette* of February 14, 1771, "Ceilings and Cornices on the shortest notice" and were but lately arrived in Annapolis from London. Their stucco work cost Lloyd £208:13:0. The obviously imported marble mantels of the parlor and dining room and the fine silver hardware are not included in the detailed entries of the ledgers.

The Buckland accounts make no mention of the hall details of the first and second floors, the beautiful door treatments of the parlor and dining room, nor the carved shutters. This must mean that Buckland carved them himself when he was again on the job in 1773 and was paid wages. The three mantels downstairs, the carving in the dining room, the cornice over the rear door and the nearly two months' work in installing them, are all mentioned. £287:4:4 was his bill, paid in 1773. The woodwork could have been made as it was installed by his shop force or by John Randall who was in his employ at an annual wage of £70. The one month and twenty days wages paid Buckland figure at about five and one half shillings a day, which is in line with wages for similar services at the time and exactly what Lloyd was to pay Noke during the better part of 1773 and 1774 after Buckland had left. For his services Buckland received the total of £303:3:8½—a not inconsiderable sum in those days.

The most conspicuous characteristic of the house is its height, more frequently seen in New England than in the middle colonies. It is a full three stories above a high basement. The exterior basement walls to the heads of the windows are stone, then to the cornice, brick laid in Flemish bond. The interior walls, the foundations of the chimneys, and the vaulting under the central hall are brick. The arches over the windows and the projecting string courses at the floor lines are rubbed brick. The roof, without dormers, is hip on hip. The width of the central hall is expressed on the street façade by a shallow projection or bay that is carried to the roof and crowned by a pediment containing a small bull's-eye window. The central window of the third story has a semi-circular head that extends pleasantly into the otherwise excessive height between the heads of the third story windows and the bed mould of the main cornice. The most prominent feature of the garden façade is the large Palladian window. The front entrance is flanked by two small windows framed by columns and pilasters with Scamozzi caps.* The main cornice has dentils and the modillions that Lloyd purchased from Chase.[14] The original kitchen was apparently in the basement. The present building in the side yard is of more recent construction for the tax list of 1798 shows no outbuildings but the stables.

The plan is the usual four room, central hall arrangement, except that there is a lateral passage between the front and back rooms. One enters directly into the hall that extends entirely through the house. The stair starts centrally in one straight flight to a landing, where it divides and continues thence in two flights to the second floor. From the landing the two side flights are cantilevered from the masonry wall enclosing the stair hall. The two portions of the lower hall are separated

---

* Scamozzi (1552-1616), North Italian architect, said to have been the first to employ the Ionic capital, with the volutes at 45°. Earlier Ionic capitals always had the volutes parallel to the entablature above.

by a screen composed of beam, Ionic columns and pilasters that repeat those flanking the entrance. The large Palladian window on the landing midway between the floors lights both levels. The interior frieze is convex and decorated with leaves, which is a motive used often by Buckland elsewhere. Architectural elaboration continues to the second floor where the closing wall is treated with central pedimented doorway

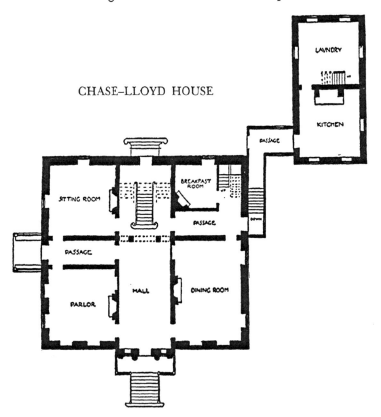

CHASE–LLOYD HOUSE

flanked by two semi-circular-headed niches. The ceiling is decorated plaster above a detailed cornice. Access to the bedrooms is through semi-circular arches. Reveals are paneled.

The doorways of the first floor are exquisite and show a sure mastery of the Georgian idiom. The trim of those in the dining room have a rope mould that ends at the base in a scroll. The upper corners have "ears." Above a frieze beautifully ornamented with a free foliated design, occurs the familiar broken pediment which in this case is supported by brackets. The doors themselves are of mahogany, six paneled, with a bead down the center to simulate a double door. The hardware is silver with drop handles on the locks, and perforated escutcheons. The inside shutters are paneled with octagons alternating with rectangles. Rosettes are in the octagonal panels in the same manner as at the Hammond house opposite. The once decorated plaster ceiling of the dining room has fallen. However, the distinctive ceiling of the parlor, low relief in the classic manner, is well preserved. The large central panel is surrounded by shallow octagonal coffers with square rosettes at the intersections of the beams.

Occupied as he was with this, his most ambitious house to date, Buckland was not happy. Life in lodgings was not satisfactory for a man with a wife and children. To add to his discomforts, it was a bitter winter, " a kind of Greenland winter " wrote the Reverend Doctor Boucher.[15] But he had made friends, and he had several most flattering offers of work in his pocket, enough to keep him busy in Annapolis for several years to come. By summer he had made up his mind to close out his Virginia shop and move it lock, stock and barrel, with his family, to this town of opportunity. With this in view he purchased a house with two lots.[16]

When Annapolis was laid out as a city in 1694, a square was reserved for the simple homes of tradesmen. It was named for the London Bloomsbury Square, an early example of town planning by the 4th Earl of Southampton only thirty years before Governor Nicholson's American project. Title to the Square was held by Charles Carroll and Governor Bladen. By 1772 another Charles Carroll divided the investment with Bladen's descendant, Daniel Dulany, and the original purpose of the place had long since been forgotten. It still consisted of the twelve half-acre lots, crossed by two streets named Carroll and Bladen for the original owners. Though accessible to church and court, it was not a fashionable part of town since the water view was obstructed by a shipyard on Dorsey's Creek. Tradesmen, too, were now forming a prosperous middle-class, living above or beside their brick shops and warehouses. Far from having a part of the town narrowly set aside for them, they had by 1772 taken over most of the town.

The Buckland lots were at the rear of a house owned by Thomas Johnson, Jr., destined to become the first elected governor of the

State.[17] Buckland did not yet aspire to a house of his own construction, but was content with an unpretentious dwelling, probably frame, for which he paid an annual ground rent of six pounds sterling for each lot. As usual, he lacked sufficient funds to buy a house as well as to pay for the move, a large outlay. It was to raise a little ready cash that he borrowed £80 from the Tappahannock merchant on his Richmond County livestock and the better part of his furniture.[18] When the list of mortgaged furnishings is checked against the pieces he owned at the time of his death it appears that many are identical. The mahogany beds, bookcase desk, walnut table, mirrors, and set of casters may have been heirlooms from the Moores. At any rate, they were valued senti- mentally, redeemed quickly from Archibald McCall and transported to their new home in Annapolis. Their livestock was reduced to two milk cows, necessary for the children.

So in September, 1772, the Buckland family was reunited. The shop was constructed on the second Bloomsbury Square lot, where, with five indentured servants and five slaves, they were now ready for business. John Randall, presumably still a member of the household, worked at an annual salary and later was made a junior partner.

Christmas was celebrated by the Buckland family with borrowed money. Mr. Faris, the genial silversmith, notes in his journal that in the course of a month William Buckland had bought wine of him, a silver watch and had borrowed £2:6 on December 22nd.[19]

The Lloyd house was nearing completion as the old year waned. The carved work for cornices, chair-rails, over-doors, and the staircase, had been delayed by the transfer of the Buckland workshop. Finishing touches were now being put on. This woodwork had taken all his craftsmen the better part of a year to create. Two months were con- sumed in the installation of it and it was April before Buckland was paid his well earned £287:4:4. His almost daily supervision was now no longer needed, and he could turn his attention to work more de- manding of his skills. Directly opposite Lloyd's house, across the narrow lane called North East Street, a new project was about to begin.

Matthias Hammond, scion of an old Anne Arundel County family, wished to have a house second to none, and one which would have personal appeal to a discriminating lady who had promised to become his wife. He left the Hammond homestead, Howard's Adventure, this winter of 1773, to be near the scene of increasing political agitation and for conferences with Mr. Buckland over his new house. The building would start with the coming of spring and good weather, for the plans were well in hand. It was to be a long, low house that would not interfere with the Lloyds' view of the bay—offices in one wing, kitchen in the other and a ball room on the second floor for the grand entertainments a Hammond might want. William Buckland worked long hours at his drawing-board to give refinement and originality to the detail. Eight chimney-pieces, all different; rosette and lozenge insets in the shutters; and a doorway that would enthrall any bride,

HAMMOND–HARWOOD HOUSE
From Journal of C. W. Peale

were among his creations. His library of English architectural books was often consulted but adaptations of the plan to the American climate and materials were of primary importance.

The Hammond house was completed in 1774. It marks the climax of Buckland's architectural career. Unlike most other houses on which it is known that he worked, this house can be attributed entirely to him as architect in the modern sense. The conception was his, the supervision of construction, and in part its execution. Let us consider the reasons for its unique distinction and why it is said to be one of the finest residences of colonial America.

As a city house, directly on a street, its setting differs from the well-known contemporary plantation houses of Maryland and Virginia which are located on large estates, approached by land through long avenues between cultivated fields or by tidal water across sloping lawns and terraced gardens. Its great distinction arises from its modesty and quiet restraint, the beauty of its proportions, the perfect relation of its five parts, and the careful workmanship and refinement of its details.

Before the encroachment of the modern city there were more extensive gardens at the rear which allowed a view of the entire composition and justified the two-story order on that façade. Here Buckland successfully solved the difficult problem of using a two-story order on residential buildings. The full traditional entablature, made up of its three parts, is too large and extremely awkward when carried around the house unsupported by either columns or pilasters at the corners and between window bays, as was done by Hoban in his design for the Executive Mansion in Washington. Buckland, not wishing such a monumental effect, omitted the two lower members, the frieze and the architrave, except over the supporting brick pilasters on the garden façade. Thus reduced, it was reconciled with the small windows and is in harmonious domestic scale. Attention is called, however, to the very skillful way in which he treats what would have been the excessive height between the heads of the second story windows and the cornice where the frieze and architrave are omitted. He introduces an elaborate window frame over the entrance which in itself becomes an element of much charm.

The brick walls are laid up in Flemish bond, one of the strongest of all the brick bonds. The classical details are well within the Georgian tradition and show the trained hand of the joiner. The cornice over the central block is enriched with dentils and modillions. The main entrance feature is beautifully proportioned and acts as a central accent to the entire composition. It was likely suggested by illustrations in the *Book of Architecture* by Gibbs, known to have been in Buckland's library, as were the delightful cartouches in the two pediments. The rusticated window on the stair landing is a copy of a window in the church of St. Martin's-in-the-Fields, London, by Gibbs and illustrated in the same book. The half-octagon bays on the wings are fairly common Georgian features and in all likelihood derive from similarly located bays on English country houses since Tudor times. An unimportant detail on the garden façade might be criticized as unarchitectural. The string course at the second floor line is unexpectedly broken around the pilasters, whereas the pilasters, as the dominant constructive feature should have been given precedence. Contemporary houses in England were usually designed by men who had started as masons and who instinctively felt the logic of construction. Buckland, trained as a joiner, in this detail betrayed his failure to sense it.

The plan is a variant of the typical Maryland plan. One enters directly into a hall that does not extend entirely through the house but only to the door of the largest room on the first floor, through which one sees the jib window on axis overlooking and giving access to the garden. This room was used as a dining room for large occasions. The stair is enclosed within its own hall through which one reaches the service wing to the right. On each side of the entrance hall is a small parlor, and in the fourth corner of the first floor is a room ·which, nearer the service, probably was a family dining room, or serving room for large dinners in the adjoining room. The other wing, having no connection through the hyphen with the main house, was used always as an office. A ballroom is located over the large room on the first floor and bedrooms occupy the other three corners of the second floor.

The interior details, entirely in the prevailing mode, are the result of Buckland's training and study of the pattern books, and the love of a colonial gentleman for the latest fashion and his willingness to incur considerable expense to obtain it. While they are elaborate they are always consistent and restrained and they show a maturity not always found in Buckland's earlier houses. There is nothing of the bizarre, sometimes exhibited by less competent designers. There is no wood paneling, no ceiling decoration nor imported marble mantels as in the Chase-Lloyd house opposite. Chair rails, window and door trim, chimney breasts and cornices are carved. The over-door treatment and the beautiful decoration of the interior shutters are especially worthy of note. The late R. T. H. Halsey in his preface to *Great Georgian Houses of America* calls attention to the striking similarity of the details of the Hammond house to those at Honington Hall in Oxfordshire: For instance, the half octagon bays on the wings, the interior shutters and window treatment. However, at Honington the trim ends in a scroll at the baseboard and at the Hammond house on the chair rail. He suggested that Buckland might have served some of his apprentice years at this Oxfordshire house. This theory is exploded, however, by the authority of H. Avery Tipping in Vol. 48 of *English Country Life*, who assigns the alterations at Honington Hall to 1744 when William Buckland was but ten years old. It is remarkable that Buckland's love of detail did not lead him to a richer stair treatment. He used the simple square baluster and the undecorated stair ends. Even in other houses attributed to him he rarely indulges in the turned and decorated baluster.

The entrance doorway is probably this house's most notable feature. Recollecting that Hammond was building for his bride to be, Buckland became almost sentimental in the decoration of this famous entrance. Festoons of roses fall gracefully in the spandrils. The slight projection of front and rear façades is carried to the roof and the crowning pediment in each case contains elaborately decorated bull's eye windows.

Like most of the young colonials in town, Matthias Hammond was restive under the restrictions which Lord Baltimore's government put upon him. For years antagonism had been building up between the upper and lower houses of the Provincial Assembly. The upper house, or Governor's Council as it was more generally called, was a small hand-picked group from the " Court Party," completely loyal to the old order and supported lavishly by the fees of office. A vehement critic of the fee system wrote to the *Gazette*, calling the Council " ten fools and one knave.[20] The Proprietary, Lord Baltimore, had an annual revenue, clear of expense, from the sale of lands, quit rents and other forms of taxation, of £12,500. Frederick, the last Lord, a dilettante and a wastrel, thought his faithful officers could stir up even more income to offset the rising expenses he could not, or would not, reduce. The faithful would not willingly yield a shilling from their own nest-feathering, though the lower house of the Assembly more than once staged a strike when important appropriations were needed. In particular were the large salaries of the clergy of the Church of England resented. These men, not always holy, were Lord Baltimore's personal appointments but were paid in tobacco from a per capita tax on every inhabitant, were he Jew, Roman Catholic or Quaker. Both Sharpe and

Eden had prorogued the Assembly when it resisted authority. Governor Eden had, furthermore, reestablished the fees of office by proclamation, thinking to avoid further controversy. At once there was a general outcry and a more detached office-holder was moved to poetry by the violence of the opposition:

> Now through the land Dissention stalks confest;
> With foul Distrust, and Hatred in her train;
> The dire infection runs from breast to breast.
> And statesmen plan—and patriots plead in vain.[21]

For months the *Maryland Gazette* carried a scholarly if heated debate between the colony's leading lawyer, Daniel Dulany of the Council, and young Charles Carroll of Carrollton, a novice in politics, who was spokesman for the liberal, independent element in the province. Their argument was over the clergy salaries. The town, divided into two camps, caused political discussions to be forbidden within any club room where some semblance of social decorum was still expected. King George demanded more and higher taxes, and so, too, did Lord Baltimore. The officers of the colony did not see the impending danger. Hammond, the grandson of one of Lord Baltimore's treasurers, took the side of Carroll and the resisting forces. He was urged to run for election to the Assembly with his friend, William Paca. Accordingly, in May, 1773, the two young men were over-whelmingly elected. It was a serious time, not conducive to house building or to courting. The first was in the able hands of William Buckland; the second suffered.

Paca, Matthias Hammond's political partner, became another of Mr. Buckland's clients. A house that had been building for over a year was ready to receive him after his election. Though he had estates on the Eastern Shore, he had decided on politics as the best way to serve his country and wished to live at the seat of government. Paca was a fine figure of a man, well over six feet, educated in England, and the inheritor of a fortune accumulated by his father, who enjoyed the confidence of the Proprietary. His own house was of a simpler plan than that of Hammond's, but he was surrounding it with one of the most pleasing gardens in Annapolis. Some years later when the Pacas had retired to their Wye Island plantation, a tenant, Rosalie Stier, daughter of a refugee Belgian baron, gave a description of the Prince

George Street dwelling: " Our house is enormously big, four rooms, below, three large and two small ones on second floor besides the staircases and the finest garden in Annapolis in which there is a spring, a cold bath house well fitted up and a running stream; what more could I ask for? " [22]

Only one room survives with its original trim. Here we find the carved shutters, similar to those in the Lloyd and Hammond houses, paneling and beautiful chimney breast and a plaster cornice of refinement. In the hall approach to one wing is a Chinese Chippendale stair-rail such as was used at Menokin. Paca employed Buckland for the interior finish of his house at the same time that he was working on the Lloyd residence. In one of the Lloyd ledgers there is a deduction for plaster " Borrowed from Mr. Paca."

Another prospective bridegroom was adding to Mr. Buckland's anxieties by demanding a quick finish to a long-projected dwelling. James Brice had inherited the lot next to William Paca's together with building materials " worked up or to be worked up." [23] Though his father, John Brice, had advertised ten years before for an undertaker who " may see the Plan," it is quite clear that he never built the house. It is probable that some earlier plan was revised by Buckland, as in the case of the Chase-Lloyd house. James Brice took his time about building and marrying. He was thirty-five years old when Julianna Jenings, daughter of the Honorable Thomas Jenings, Attorney General, consented to be his bride. They were married in 1781, many years after the house was finished. An oft repeated story to the effect that Jenings built the house as a wedding present to his daughter is certainly not verified by John Brice's 1766 will, nor by a 1773 advertisement in the *Maryland Gazette* of a " tavern on East Street a few doors below Mr. Brice's new house." There is some evidence, however, that James Brice had earlier expectations of carrying a bride across his threshold but that the romance went amiss. [24] This would account for the completion of the large and handsome dwelling eight years before his wedding.

The distinguishing feature of the house is the very high gable roof—as high as the house from grade to cornice—and the towering chimneys. The front and rear bricks are laid all headers with vertical joints broken. The main cornice is most unusual and with the central window of the second story partakes of the nature of furniture. Little arches are supported on turned balusters which together make the frieze. The window is too crowded and it and the trivial detail of the cornice are " fussy." They remind one of the fact that Buckland served his uncle, the joiner, as apprentice and that he made and sold furniture. Perhaps he put the finishing touches on the exterior details of the Brice house. The interior details are much nearer the sure and fully developed style of Buckland, and they illustrate his familiarity with the best Georgian prototype. Although the ends of the stair treads are beautifully carved above a complicated fret, the stair rail has the simple

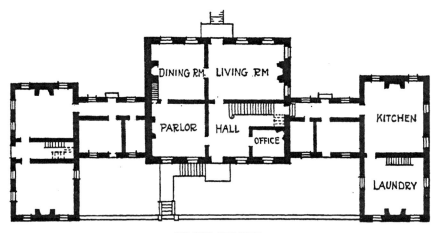

BRICE HOUSE

square baluster seen in most of Buckland's houses. The splendid parlor chimney-breast was undoubtedly inspired by Plate 50 in Swan's *British Architect*. The parlor cornice is the most elaborate and highly decorated of all the Maryland houses. The bed mould, the cyma, and the modillions are carved. The frieze is convex and decorated with oak leaves and acorns. The mantel has not escaped, in recent times, the addition of an extra shelf to give greater projection for mantel ornaments, now thought necessary. The break of the plaster paneling around the projection of the door cornice is awkward and unarchitectural.

It is interesting to note that each of these houses, built about the same time, has original features. To be sure they are all large city houses, all are of brick, all but the Lloyd house have a central block with connecting wings, and all have interior woodwork from the Buckland drawing board and shop. All had cross drafts so necessary in hot weather, and all had the service areas as far as possible from the main section of the house. But each house has its own individuality. Buckland did repeat his designs and motives occasionally, but not in these houses, practically adjoining. The treatment of the stairs varies, as does the shape and size of the wings and hyphens, the placing and pattern of chimneys and the carving of the mantels. His plasterers introduced variety in the stucco designs as did his carvers in the embellishment executed on local pine and cypress, or imported mahogany. Each owner had impressed his personality on Buckland who in turn created for each an elegant setting. Each house has a distinctive, decorative window, either at the front or the rear. Each has beautiful interior detail.

As Buckland's reputation grew he was sought out as arbiter and expert witness in legal cases growing out of building disputes. Twice in the August Court of Anne Arundel County was he called to testify. In one of these cases he was given the official title of " architect." [25] The eighteenth century was reluctant to confer professional titles except in the case of the military. There were few able-bodied gentlemen in Maryland or Virginia who did not acquire the prefix " Colonel " for life, but Doctors and Reverends raised suspicion and demanded proof. The Governor's Council and other bigwigs of official colonial life could rate an " Honrbl." The British caste system still guided the colonists in being respectful to the handful of belted knights resident in the new world, but any large landowner could be an " Esquire " and all other white men except indentured servants were called " Mister." In Maryland and Virginia there were no " Judges," no " Admirals " and by this time, 1773, no Indian Chiefs. The term " architect," as we have seen, was one that had to be earned by skill and reputation. Buckland was an able draftsman, a master carpenter and joiner, a student of Swan, Gibbs, Langley and Morris, a man of taste with a creative mind. He was an architect. Also at this time, he is recorded in a deed as " Gentleman." [26]

When William Eddis wrote his friend in England a description of Maryland and of the Annapolitans he added that " an idea of equality also seems to prevail and the inferior order of people pay but little external respect to those who occupy superior stations." [27] He was thinking more of the townspeople, possibly, than of the really inferior third-class citizens, the indentured servants. However, rebellion was rife and Mr. Buckland, among others, was having difficulty in holding his laborers. Some of his Virginia men had worked out their time and new ones had been purchased in Maryland. The first to give him trouble was Thomas Hoskins, a bricklayer " lately imported " in the *Lovely Kitty* of Captain Collwell Howard, who ran away in September.[28] Hoskins seems to have succeeded in eluding the law as his name does not appear again in the Buckland record. In the days of no insurance, runaways could be disastrous to business. The escape of Hoskins made a total loss to his employer of about twenty pounds, his purchase price, not to mention the setback to whatever building was in progress. Even more valuable to his master was Thomas Hall, a carver, who ran away in December. One of the original London carvers of whom Buckland had boasted to Robert Carter, he had served his time " but executed another indenture, by which he was to be allowed in consideration of his former services, wages at the rate of 10 shillings per week till the expiration of his time which would have been in September Next." This man had been happy in his work with Buckland, had risen in his service, was able to dress well, wear silver shoebuckles and have his hair " curled at the ears and clubbed behind," but saw his chance to disappear into the American countryside and took it.[29]

Still more disastrous to any commission must have been the vanishing of a plasterer and two bricklayers, advertised for in a Baltimore newspaper that November. Buckland signed the advertisement with one Thomas Price, a leading citizen of Frederick County.[30] The fact that this notice appeared in a Baltimore paper with circulation in the northern counties, rather than in the *Gazette* published in Annapolis, leads one to believe that the men ran away from work in that area. Strangely there is no mention of the place to which they are to be returned " where £5 and reasonable charges will be paid." Rewards, no doubt, could be arranged through the management of the newspaper, but the advertisement implies that both signers were well-known throughout the province. Price was a justice of the County Court, a trustee of the Free School, and a man on whom his fellow countians later bestowed many other positions of trust. It is known that he built a handsome dwelling house in Frederick Town on the Court House

Square, a house that was long ago demolished to make way for the Episcopal church. From this evidence of runaway workmen it appears that he was building it in November, 1773, and that William Buckland had a hand in it. One of the three runaways was returned, as his name appears later in the inventory of Buckland's estate.

In these prewar years, there was scarcely a lot in Annapolis that did not have signs of building on it. Young Mr. Ogle was adding an octagonal wing to the house his father, the Governor, had lived in many years earlier. The sporting Mr. Lloyd Dulany, distinctly of the Court Party and yet an intimate of Colonel George Washington, was building a three-story mansion, so that he could gaze over roofs as well as his cousin, Colonel Lloyd. Perhaps Mr. Buckland could furnish them with plans? All the wealthy wanted to be fashionable except Miss Elizabeth Bordley, whose home was comfortable enough for an elderly spinster waiting to join her youthful lover in another world. Governor Eden was entertaining merrily in his completed mansion. The Ball Room was in constant use. The new theatre was a great success. Around the harbor merchants were erecting larger places of business.[31]

Buckland was certainly working to the limits of his endurance and capacity on the five residences, yet he was able to enter, also, into a field of a more public character. In March of the previous year he had joined the throng on the hill to witness the laying of the corner stone of the new Stadt House. Governor Eden had made a graceful little speech; there were " loyal and constitutional toasts given at the cold collation that followed; " ringing cheers from the artisans, accompanied by claps of unseasonable thunder.[32] Some took it as an omen that the Stadt House would never be built, but these were not the friends of Charles Wallace, the undertaker, a public-spirited merchant with energy and resourcefulness. A committee of six had been appointed to supervise. Wallace, one of the supervisors, had volunteered to be the contractor. Plans and estimates had been advertised for without success because the Assembly's paltry £7,000 did not tempt architects or builders. In the Act, provision had been made for designing rooms for the upper and lower houses of the Assembly, for court rooms, jurors' rooms, committee rooms, offices and a repository for records. When the advertisement brought no answers, Wallace went on alone. He used, in all likelihood, a design drawn by Joseph Horatio Anderson, a local architect, and handed out contracts to various joiners and merchants. By June the work had progressed to the point of roofing, but the Assembly disagreed on whether the building should be covered with shingles or copper.[33] Copper was finally favored, but this required another appropriation for the extra cost and a long delay while it was found and shipped from England. It was obvious that the interior could not be installed until the building was properly covered. We know, however, that the upper rooms were finished and the copper roof on when, in September, 1775, a hurricane struck.[34] Off came the roof and the crumpled metal, blown down the hill, became useful only as war salvage.

As late as 1779 there were disputes about the amounts of money due Wallace, as the Assembly claimed his work had " more elegance than was required by contract . . . in the doors, the Great Hall, and the Senate House." [35] Thus Wallace's public-spirited enterprise resulted in personal sacrifice. It is likely that Wallace employed Buckland for some interior work and that Buckland had contributed the extra elegance of the doors and Senate Room. There is documentary evidence in the State Archives that Buckland was paid £25 for " his expenses and services relative to the Public Building in this City." [36] Based on his previous pay for plans this would have been a fair return for submitting detailed drawings of the woodwork to be installed.

The Senate Chamber is a large square room of dignified proportions. It has a low wainscot and modillioned plaster cornice. Across one end is a visitors' gallery supported on four Ionic columns with Scamozzi caps. On the opposite side of the room, as a background for the Speaker's desk, is a semi-circular niche below a pediment. The rail of the gallery, except where the central pediment breaks up into it, has turned balusters. The doors, windows and fireplace are framed with the conventional architrave moulding.

The chronology of the State House makes it clear that Buckland never saw his work installed. There is only the evidence of family lore, lore written into memoirs to be sure, that places the finishing of the Senate Chamber in the hands of John Randall. Randall told his children that, after the death of his guardian and business partner, he had with his own hands helped set the fluted columns supporting the ladies' gallery. So firmly fixed was this idea in the mind of one child that from pure sentiment he bought in one of the pillars when the old Senate Chamber was completely " renovated " in 1878.[37] Since subcontractors' accounts were not kept in the State Archives there will probably never be more evidence than at present. Only one other bill was ever submitted by Buckland to the Province of Maryland and that is one included in the accounts of the Commissioner of the Land Office. In the year 1774, Buckland's shop made a large double office desk for £15 and repaired a table.[38] This was another occasion when the joiners turned their tools to the delicate work of furniture making, an art in which Annapolis was to secure some small fame.

VII

Last Years

WILLIAM BUCKLAND found in 1773 an opportunity to retrace his steps from Annapolis to Fairfax County, Virginia. Bernard Sears, the builder who had worked with him fifteen years before, asked his help on the interior of the new Pohick Church rising at the crossroads on the highway to Alexandria. The original " undertaker," Daniel French, the same man who had known Ariss and Buckland in Richmond County, died suddenly, leaving George Mason his executor. Wishing to clear his friend's estate of his business involvements and because he was a vestryman of Truro Parish, Mason consented to act as contractor to finish the church. Tradition has it that Colonel George Washington, with his exactness and engineering skill had selected a site more nearly at the parish's population center than that of the old church. He had also drawn, it is said, a sketch to scale to guide the builder. Work progressed slowly, but by the end of 1773 the pine paneling, pulpit and chancel had been installed. The pews were sold to parishioners from 1772 to 1774.[1]

Attribution of Buckland's work here rests not solely on the fact that he was known to French, Mason and Sears but on a statement made by an eye-witness that at the top of one of the Ionic pilasters forming part of the ornamental work of the chancel was incised into the wood " 1773 W. B., sculptor." [2] When the church was restored in 1906 the old woodwork had to be entirely replaced and the inscription was lost. We have only one man's word for this signature, but it was accepted by a Bishop! Sears was paid £58:19:0 for the carving when the interior was complete. This would have covered his own as well as his sub-contractor's work.

Pohick, four years in building, is the usual rectangular country church but larger than most. The chancel, high pulpit under a canopy, gallery and box pews are handsomely designed and show restraint and dignity. The altarpiece with the Creed and Lord's Prayer was, according to the vestry records, to be picked out in gold leaf supplied by Colonel Washington. Since the interior was carefully restored through study of the old vestry books, one can judge it as it stands, and it is a credit to Buckland and his associates.

It is certain that Buckland would have wanted to show his best work to Colonel Mason, his first patron. Probably executed in the Annapolis shop, the woodwork was most likely brought by boat to the Gunston Hall landing or even farther up the creek. Overseeing the installation would have required the personal attention of the architect. Did he, Mason's former indentured servant, now " gent.", spend a night at Gunston? Did he chance to hear his former master discourse on the rights of the colonies or the necessity for war? Buckland would have been welcome, not only for himself or hospitality's sake, but also for what news he brought from the largest town between Philadelphia and Charleston. We can be sure that an evening or two was well spent in conversation and that this contact with old associates meant much to him.

Back in Annapolis the busy architect had little or no time for the diversions which were part of the charm of the town. The card club was meeting once a week at Mrs. Howard's Coffee House where large sums were exchanged by the sporting element. The town wits gathered at the Homony Club to propound droll verse or extemporaneous puns. The more serious minded, though often the same citizens on a less relaxed evening, debated at the Forensic Club such timely questions as " Whether the people have a right to dethrone a King who degenerates into a Tyrant." [3] All these entertaining occupations were accompanied by bowls of punch and indulged in by the male members only of the community. A close scrutiny of the surviving lists of members does not reveal the name of William Buckland. Faris records in his daybook the mild dissipation of two " toddeys " only, served Buckland in 1773 and 1774.[4] His lack of club life was not due to his being socially unqualified, or unpopular, for he was of a friendly and genial nature. Rather it was that he was burning the candle at both ends by his frequent business trips outside the city, his long evenings at the drafting board, his teaching untrained laborers his meticulous standards.

As the year 1774 progressed Mr. Buckland was harassed by the running away of other workmen. A Maryland spring with its riot of beauty induces unrest. Two joiners and two plasterers, one of them Richard Sadler, who had only recently been returned from his previous wanderings, went off in March and April.[5] The record does not show that they were ever returned. John Randall, who had ridden up from Virginia with his one little inherited Negro boy in attendance, now boasted an indentured joiner of his own. This man, too, disappeared in June.[6] This was more than discouraging in the face of all the work they had on hand to finish. But the future as far as new work was concerned, grew daily more ominous.

The left-wing colonists, among whom were Chase, Paca and Hammond, advocated not only an embargo on British goods but also a moratorium on the paying of debts. The conservatives realized that such action was both dishonest and stifling to future credit and trade. Both sides agreed, however, that " the suffering of Boston is in the general cause of America and that union and mutual confidence is the basis on which our common liberties can only be supported." [7] After the more zealous patriots met and signed an agreement to make it illegal to collect British debts in Maryland, it was noised about town that the agreement had passed with a bare majority. The conservatives promptly held a meeting to denounce the one of the previous day, and in signing the new proclamation left their names to posterity.[8] Here is the entire list of office holders under the Crown and Lord Baltimore, men later termed Loyalists or Tories as the case might be, as well as the substantial merchants and professional men who believed in paying debts. Among the latter were Buckland's two intimates, John Randall and Denton Jacques. The architect, William Buckland, did not sign. There were probably men who could not bring themselves to sign either declaration. Many of Buckland's wealthy patrons were still undecided in their views, wishfully thinking that they could have local independence and still be loyal to the King. Seemingly calm, but weighted with anxiety, Governor Eden was writing letters to his superiors. He described the logical conclusions of the late British policy and begged for reassurance as to the future. The Boston Port Bill was one answer; the drilling of county militia was another.

There was little tobacco going to England and few imports were arriving at the docks. Only the rich with their credit and reserves could force a smile. Old finery was beginning to look shabby. The country people bragged of their homespun clothes. In the neighborhood of markets new businesses were springing up in an attempt to manufacture goods to supplant the missing importations. An enterprising Annapolis man showed patriotism by opening a stocking factory. On each ankle, in place of the clock, was spelled out the word AMERICA.[9] Quick fortunes were in store for the clever. But the big business of overseas trade was at a standstill, and merchants fortunate enough to own plantations retired to them.

Perhaps Mr. Buckland did not relish the idea of maintaining more indentured servants in such unpromising times and so did not replenish his shop force. He could always pick up a journeyman or two in town. The taxable items, glass, nails, paint and hardware of various sorts which were in short supply, could not now be imported, thus hampering building. Those Sons of Liberty, Mr. Hammond and Mr. Paca, were much too busy to give thought to their houses. Mr. Brice was recruiting a militia company. In the lull before the storm Buckland remembered the portrait he had promised Mr. Peale that he would sit for. In his new status of gentleman, a portrait was a necessity. Whether he returned to England or remained in Maryland he could not hope to get a better likeness for the small outlay of ten pounds.

It is thought that Charles Willson Peale and Buckland were friends. There is certainly not much evidence of it in Peale's diary. Years later he speaks of " Mr. Buckley " in a vague way as a friend of Mr. Sprigg's rather than as a friend of his own. But the two clever men must have been thrown together on many occasions in Annapolis, where their acquaintances and interests were mutual. Buckland sat for him, probably in the spring of 1774, but Peale, in his haste to arrange sittings for other clients, left the background and figure to be filled in at a later time. His diary records that Mr. Buckland's portrait was not finished until April, 1787, when it was left at Mr. Callahan's in Annapolis.[10]

This portrait is one of the most successful of Peale's early work. He has made his subject alive. It is of a virile, slender man with a sensitive face and artistic long hands. He wears his own hair, arranged much as was his runaway carver's who probably copied the master, " curled over the ears and clubbed behind." His dress is simple and dignified, in shades of brown. On the table by his side are a case of drawing instruments, the tools of his profession, with the floor plan of the Hammond house, the proof of his calling. The background, too, depicts the elements of the architect's vocation, the classical portico and scaffolding. Peale, possibly remembering Kneller's portrait of the great Wren, used a similar pose and background when depicting his only architect sitter. He has painted an animated man, interested in his profession, responsive to the artist, a handsome man in full vigor.

In June, while Peale was paying his second visit to Mount Vernon to paint Colonel Washington, a general convention of representatives from the Maryland counties met in Annapolis to choose delegates to a proposed Congress and to carry on the increasingly difficult public business. When July came the Post Office advertised unclaimed letters, among them some for William Buckland.[11] This had happened once or twice before when it is likely that the addressee was absent on a business trip. Since postage was paid at the receiving end, the man to whom the letters were addressed was obviously not around to claim them. Buckland, unlike Francis Lightfoot Lee, would have had no objections to paying the postage. Lee, impervious to inconvenience, inserted a notice in the *Virginia Gazette* for May 16, 1766, which read, " The subscriber requests it as a Favour of all his Acquaintances, That they will never take any Letter directed to him out of the P. O. as he is determined never willingly to pay a Farthing of any Tax laid upon this Country, in an unconstitutional Manner."

As a hot summer progressed, William Buckland made another one of those mysterious business deals that became imbedded in the surviving records of Anne Arundel County. On August 11 he borrowed £296:18:1, current money, from a local merchant, James Williams, on the security of his house and two lots in Bloomsbury Square and his five Negro slaves.[12] The mortgage was to run only until November, a matter of three months. Was he in some business difficulty because he had been unable to collect sums owing him for the many houses on which he was working? Large debts do not show up in his final court accounts, only small amounts due him from Mr. Hammond and Mr. Brice. We know that Colonel Lloyd had made full payment for his house in the previous year. Was a new piece of business in the air which required capital? Was he planning another move? Or was he still careless in business?

Blood was shed in Boston and General Gage was cursed heartily by everyone up and down the coast. In accordance with a resolution passed by a determined Congress, Maryland decreed that amusements were to cease—no races, no balls, no theatre, and very little jovial fellowship at the clubs. Buckland's opportunities to design and construct handsome dwellings for the well-to-do vanished. Architecture and elaborate joinery gave way to shipbuilding, feverishly undertaken for lack of American bottoms. The Assembly saw to it that the copper roof was on the " new Stadt House," passed an act to raise funds for a new church in Annapolis, " it being too small inconvenient and in a ruinous State," and adjourned not to meet again until 1777.[13] British ships lay idle at their berths, chariots and chairs ceased their rounds of warehouses, shops and taverns. Grim-faced citizens counted their stores, their rapidly shrinking credit and their unsalable hogsheads of tobacco. Those fortunate few who possessed " hard money " held on to it. The *Gazette* ran a column on the making of gunpowder. Children played soldier in the streets and the whistling of martial airs fell on the ear. William Buckland probably had no heart to fight against his native land and if he stayed on in Maryland, what else could he do? Sooner or later he would be forced to take an oath of allegiance, if he did not first shoulder a musket. He was forty years old with a family to support. He borrowed money for some emergency. One possibility is that he, like so many others, planned to return to England.

More terrifying than all the tales of oppression in New England, because it was closer to home, was an event which took place in Annapolis that October.[14] A brig, the *Peggy Stewart*, arrived in port and was discovered to have on board a consignment of 2,300 pounds of tea directed to the firm of Thomas C. Williams & Co., one of whose partners was the man who held the Buckland mortgage. Anthony Stewart, Esq., the owner of the brig, without consulting anyone, least of all the Committee of Correspondence which had assumed virtual control of government in the colony, paid duty on " the Obnoxious weed " in order to release the cargo. He professed innocence as to motive. The Williamses swore they knew nothing of the tea. The captain took oath that it was on board without his knowledge, and nobody to this day knows who gave away the secret. But buried in the business letters of the largest mercantile firm in Annapolis is the following statement, written August 4, 1774, by Joshua Johnson, the London partner:

> I should not be surprised to hear that you made a BonFire of the Peggy Stewart as I have a hint that a certain T. W. [Thomas Williams] has shipped Tea on Board of her and that Captain Jackson applied to old Russell and told him that he was suspicious of it but Russell told him it was not his Business so that he got the 2½% of Freight. Russell satisfied him by telling him it was Linens. I am suspicious that it was done up in that way to deceive; if he has been hardy enough to do so daring a thing I hope that you will adopt a proper punishment for him and the old Rascall who was active in the affair.[15]

If this letter arrived before the *Peggy Stewart* docked it served as the match for the bonfire which took place on October 19th. The owner having made no peace by abject apology, and confronted by a threatening mob, burned ship and cargo with his own hand. Presumably William Buckland stood at the foot of the Governor's garden with several hundred of his fellow citizens to watch this handsome craft blaze and smoulder off Windmill Point.

After five months in England, Governor Eden returned to Annapolis. "The Governor is returned to a land of trouble," reported Eddis. "The universal cry is Liberty." [16] The *Gazette* was still occupied with the aftermath of the *Peggy Stewart* affair. Even the Court Party was frightened and less sure of its future. Great decisions were expected to emanate from the Congress still sitting in Philadelphia. Eden and his followers waited for what they hoped would be a return to reason.

But if William Buckland could not leave the country, his family still must eat. Another possible reason why he borrowed 300 pounds on the security of his property in Annapolis was to undertake what would have been the largest project of his professional career. On November 8th the *Gazette* carried an advertisement for bids on building a court house on the Eastern Shore. A new county, made by dividing Talbot and Queen Anne's Counties, had been named Caroline for

Mrs. Eden, sister of Frederick, Lord Baltimore. A site was picked for the county seat where the Court House was to be erected:

> The trustees for building a court house and prison in Caroline County, do hereby give notice that they will attend Melville's Warehouse on the 16th and 17th days of the present instant, November, in order to agree with workmen to execute the same agreeable to plans and elevations that will be produced, which plans etc. may be seen at any time between this and the 16th by applying to William Buckland in Annapolis.[17]

The editor's timeworn copy of this issue has William Buckland's name in ink across the advertisement, showing that he personally authorized it.

The Commissioners bought land for the public buildings and decided that a new town to be erected around them should be called Eden Town. The cost of the building was not to exceed 70,000 pounds of tobacco, a large sum.[18] Much time was consumed by disputes about the site, and when the approaching war turned men's minds to other matters, the building project was postponed. The court house was not built until 1795, whether after Buckland's plans we do not know. It had a good classical doorway, pediment with a bulls-eye window and a cornice with modillions.[19] Eden Town became Edenton and finally Denton and the handsome brick Court House with symmetrical two-story wings was taken down to make way for the present one.

On the 16th of November William Buckland was active in his profession. A month later he was dead. At the height of his career, a man with talents so needed in the development of a new country, a man who but a few months before when his portrait was painted looked in the best of health, vanished from the scene. The *Gazette* did not give his death a single line. There are no records of epidemics at this time, though in the previous year " hundreds in Maryland had been carried off by Putrid Quinzy."[20] Certainly Buckland died of no lingering or congenital ailment, but suddenly. Newspapers of the day were quite as conscious as they are today of public interest in the more lurid news. Death notices were restricted to a line or two for the prominent only and usually some time after the burial. It seems certain that his death took place on the Eastern Shore. If he had attended the meeting of the trustees of the court house, at Melville's Warehouse, on November

16th, as he was most certain to do, he was there stricken. In those days people were buried where they died so there would be no record of burial in St. Anne's cemetery, Annapolis, at that time the church yard. The lone entry for funeral expenses involved Isaac Greentree who was a deputy Commissary for Queen Anne's County, a position similar to Judge of the Orphan's Court, and the ten pounds received from the estate for the funeral would have amply covered service and fees.[21] Authority was granted by the December Anne Arundel Court to appraisers and to Buckland's executors. Since he died intestate, Mary Buckland, the widow, John Randall and Denton Jacques were named administrators by the court and bonded for the sum of 2,000 pounds sterling, a large bond.[22]

The first public notice of the death of a man who was known from Tidewater Virginia to the foothills of the Blue Ridge in Maryland, was that of the almost immediate sale of all the Buckland shop force, with "a parcel of household furnishings." Two bricklayers, a painter, a carver and a stonemason were sold, together with five country-born Negroes who had accompanied the family up from Virginia.[23] It is interesting to note that Oxford, the man who had been bought with the Richmond County farm, was valued at sixty pounds, Buckland's single most valuable chattel. Mary Buckland and the other two executors made a quick decision to disband the office and shop force and be freed of the expense of maintaining ten extra souls. Actually, Mary may have bought back some of the slaves, and John Randall some of the workmen, for life had to go on. The widow and children remained in the Bloomsbury Square house until it, too, was sold at public vendue on June 26, 1775.[24] The house and lots were bought by Daniel Wells.[25] Where Mary Buckland lived after this, we do not know. That she remained in Annapolis is evident, for five years later, her eldest daughter, Mary, became the wife of George Mann, the owner and genial host of the best hostelry in town. Sarah, the second daughter, also made a good marriage in Annapolis. Of Francis, the son, who with his sister Sarah signed the inventory, we hear no more, and it is assumed that he died young.[26]

The inventory of the estate is the most important document pertaining to this story, for on it is based much of the detail of William Buckland's life and works.[27] It proves that he combined with his original joinery, the practical aspects of " undertaking," contracting, and actual construction. It proves that he was a designer and a man of taste and culture. Here we see his capital investment in skilled workers, in tools, in building materials such as lumber, bricks, lime, hair, glue, sash glass. There are evidences of the refinements of his profession, his drawing boards and paper, his mathematical instruments, gold leaf, mahogany, two elaborate " ornamented paper ceilings " valued at ten pounds. But the most impressive items in the inventory are his books, fifteen expensive standard volumes on architecture, design and carving. There are, also on his library list, two books of sermons, a three-volume *Dictionary of Arts & Sciences*, and thirteen volumes of lighter reading, besides a parcel of magazines. It was no small achievement for a man in his position to acquire in the course of nineteen years a library of about forty books.[28] How and where he collected them remains a conjecture. Although William Aikman's circulating library and book store in Annapolis was a source of supply for the whole colony during the years 1773-1774, and gentlemen's libraries were frequently auctioned, orders for books from England were customary.

It is possible to visualize the Bucklands' home life by studying the contents of the inventory. The Bloomsbury Square residence was probably a story and a half edifice, with seven rooms. Heated by open fires in at least two well-equipped fireplaces, lit by candle light, it was a compact, well furnished dwelling. There would have been no individual water systems in the Square, but rather a communal well to which the Buckland servants went with the two well buckets. The kitchen, usually semi-detached in Annapolis, was well stocked with copper and iron cooking utensils and stores of soap, oil, hog's fat, and spices. Whether a bit of tea was treasured in the mahogany tea chest one can only surmise. This room held, also, a walnut dining table and walnut sideboard. The living room, which served as formal dining room too, contained another dining table, but of mahogany, six mahogany chairs, a tea table and the handsomest piece they owned, a mahogany desk and bookcase, the same piece listed when the furniture was mortgaged in Virginia. An office for the architect and the master bedroom would have completed the arrangement of the ground floor. On the second floor would have been two large bedrooms, dormitories we would call them. Beds were made for sharing in those days and were often expected to give a comfortable night's rest to three people! The inventory lists as bedroom furnishings five complete beds with sheets, blankets and counterpanes, besides a cradle, servant's bed and sundry odd mattresses and linens. There are also one mahogany chest of drawers, three arm chairs and several chests which served as both clothes closet and chair. The luxuries are few; a large and a small looking glass, silver which consists of spoons, a caster-set and a watch, account for all. Pewter and earthenware were in daily use. Mary Buckland's industry is attested by a spinning-wheel and quilting frame, and she it was who probably used the "tin garden waterer" in attempts to beautify her yard.

The other building on the lot contained the shop. The five slaves would have slept on the second floor of this house. Here the assessor intimates disorder about the premises for he twice mentions planks and scantling "lying about the lots and building."

Through the three years following Buckland's death the executors, John Randall and Denton Jacques, brought in their administrative accounts to the Anne Arundel County Court.[29] In these is bared the business life of a professional man. Buckland owed money on two personal bonds (required of a builder) and two debts to Lord Baltimore's Loan Office, the bank of the day. A judgment was obtained against the estate by Richard MacKubin, a merchant who sold paint and glass. Lancelot Jacques, Denton's uncle and a prominent Annapolis merchant, signed the inventory as a creditor, as did James Williams, the holder of the mortgage, but while Williams is recorded as being paid, there is no further mention of Lancelot Jacques. On the other side of the ledger, Bennet Chew, Charles Roberts and William Waller owed the estate. Except for small items that appear in the testamentary account, "for so much gained by finishing Mr. Hammond's House, £96:17:6" and "Received from Mr. Brice for work done to the time of sale, deducting for board and maintenance of the servant," Buckland's work was ended. Denton Jacques left Annapolis to develop his uncle's iron mines and forge in Frederick County. John Randall took over what business was left on the Buckland books until the call to arms came to him, as it did to other young Annapolitans by 1776.

For the one hundred and fifty years following William Buckland's death his name was lost in the annals of Annapolis. It had never been remembered elsewhere. His memory was kept alive, if not green, in two or three families who had a personal interest in him. His daughters, Mary Mann and Sarah Callahan, left many taciturn descendants. Among these the Harwoods were able to state that their house had been built by " a Mr. Buckland " but even they had forgotten his Christian name.[30] It is always permissible to select for adulation one's most distinguished ancestors. Thus the Harwoods honored their Harwood and Chase forbears and put their inherited portrait of William Buckland into the dark recesses of an attic and out of mind. The Randall family cherished a tradition of grandfather John's brief foray into the world of art and architecture, firm in the knowledge of a few facts, and owners of a few Buckland documents. But no one knew who Buckland was and cared less. Only with increasing interest in the origins of our national culture, in the history and restoration of old houses, in the ferreting out the records of men of lesser stature who helped create our cultural heritage, has the story of pioneers like William Buckland seemed important.

With no descendants of his name, no fortune, and few followers, William Buckland at the age of forty left his mark on American domestic architecture. Most of his monuments still stand as strong as the day he built them, monuments that immortalize the taste of the eighteenth century gentleman and the skill of a colonial craftsman.

RINGGOLD HOUSE. Chimney breast and wall treatment show an extreme delicacy and refinement in the manner of Grinling Gibbons. (Now in the Baltimore Museum of Art.)

Buckland's cipher and the date on reverse of paneling.

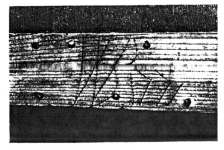

CHASE-LLOYD HOUSE. The semi-circular headed
entrance, flanked by windows and engaged columns, is
a most unusual combination of architectural features.

Palladian window that lights the stair on
the rear façade of the Chase-Lloyd House.

Chase-Lloyd House.
Elaborately detailed
second floor hall.

Exquisite doorway that shows Buckland's talent in its full development

Screen dividing entrance hall from stair, the stair of cantilevered construction, and the Palladian window.

THE HAMMOND-HARWOOD HOUSE, built by Matthias Hammond, Buckland's finest achievement. In the beauty of its proportions and details it is unrivaled in the thirteen colonies.

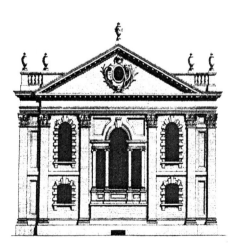

East façade of St.-Martin's-in-the-Fields, London, from Gibbs' book which served as inspiration for many of Buckland's details.

Entrance to the Hammond-Harwood house. Earlier steps and rail were of wood.

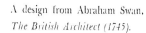

A design from Abraham Swan, *The British Architect* (1745).

Dining room at the Hammond-Harwood house
showing complete mastery of the Georgian idiom.

Garden side of the Hammond-Harwood house. The full architectural order here was used also at Whitehall as a free portico.

The jib window that gives access to the garden.

SARAH CALLAHAN, Buckland's daughter, and her
daughter Anne, painted by Charles Willson Peale, 1791.

Sally and Polly, children of
John and Sarah Callahan.

Street front of the PACA HOUSE.

Surviving parlor with
carved mantel, cornice
and window shutters.

THE BRICE HOUSE. The steep roof, tall chimneys
and wide-spread plan, in spite of severity of detail,
give the house great distinction. The steps are modern.

Chimney breast which includes many of
the motives taken from the pattern books.

Interior cornice in the Brice house in which Buckland used his favorite oak leaf and acorn convex frieze and modillions.

Stair ends and string course, carved with spirit and grace, show Buckland's skill as a joiner.

A chimney breast from Abraham Swan's book. Compare
with those of Hammond-Harwood and Brice houses.

THE SENATE CHAMBER of the State House at
Annapolis, showing speaker's dais as restored in 1905.
The room was authentically refurnished in 1941.

Washington resigning his commission, December 23, 1783, in the Senate Chamber, painted by John Trumbull in 1817. Trumbull shows the Ladies' Gallery but took liberties with the architectural arrangement.

Annapolis. E.U.

Watercolor of Annapolis from Strawberry Hill painted by a French officer in 1797. At left is the old windmill on Windmill Point on the Annapolis side of the Severn River. The next clearly visible building is the old Governor's Mansion. In the center are the closely grouped Ogle, Hammond-Harwood and Chase-Lloyd houses. To right is the Liberty poplar and the the original building of St. John's College. Next is the State House with its dome. Bloomsbury Square is in the foreground and at extreme right St. Anne's Church with square steeple.

VIII

Postscript

IT IS AMAZING that the intervening two hundred years have not destroyed William Buckland's work. His houses, built for the most part of substantial brick, have with one or two exceptions survived. His pine paneling, his plaster cornices, his mahogany stair rails, have escaped the ravages of insects, dampness and fire. Possibly because even the country houses were convenient to towns or adaptable to modern living they have seldom been without tenants. Only the glebe houses of Truro and Lunenburg parishes, the jail and work-house of Richmond County, all in Virginia, and Strawberry Hill, his one wood residence near Annapolis, have disappeared. Five out of a pretty well authenticated twenty-two is a remarkably small proportion.

Gunston Hall passed from the Mason family through many hands to the happy ownership of Mr. and Mrs. Louis P. Hertle. They restored the house and gardens and bequeathed it to the State of Virginia but to be perpetually cared for by the National Society of Colonial Dames. Beautifully furnished, this masterpiece of William Buckland's youth may be seen for a fee. The entrance is to the east of U. S. Route 1 not far from Pohick Church.

Pohick Church, because of its historic associations, was restored in 1906 and again occupies an important place in the Protestant Episcopal Diocese of Virginia. After the Revolution it was seldom used and fell into disrepair. The interior was ruined when the building was occupied by Union troops, using it as a stable, during the Civil War. Because the vestry books giving details of building and design are preserved the task of restoration was simplified. The church stands close to the highway, U. S. 1, about thirteen miles south of Alexandria.

Rockledge, sometimes known as The Den, is still a private residence. Its view of the old mills and Occoquan Creek is almost as it was in Ballendine's day. The road to it turns west at Woodbridge off U. S. Route 1.

Down the Northern Neck of Virginia on Va. Route 3 one comes in about sixty miles from Fredericksburg to Warsaw, formerly Richmond Court House. Here still stands the little Clerk's Office next to a more modern Court House and nearby is a building which may be Buckland's gaol. Five miles toward the Rappahannock river are the gates to Sabine Hall on the one side and those of Mount Airy on the other. Sabine Hall has long been the seat of the Wellford family who inherited it through their descent from the Carters. Mount Airy, too, remains a family treasury of furniture and portraits. The estate, still farmed and lived in by Tayloes, upholds its reputation as one of the great American residences of the eighteenth century.

Menokin is a neglected house. Though the acres are farmed, the house is so far removed from the main road that access on the overgrown private road is almost impossible. No one lives there and even its sturdy construction can not long survive the elements.

Across the Rappahannock in Essex County lie Blandfield and Elmwood. Both are on U. S. Route 17 out of the picturesque county seat, Tappahannock. Blandfield has never been out of the Beverley family, its broad acres still under cultivation by a Robert of that name. Elmwood is ten miles farther on, near Loretto. This lovely place suffered neglect after the Civil War but is once again in the sympathetic hands of a Garnett.

William Buckland came from Virginia to Maryland a mature and experienced man. As the exact period of his work on some of the country mansions is unknown, they will be mentioned according to their proximity to Virginia. Montpelier, not far from Laurel, was a Snowden seat for many years but is now owned by the Hon. Breckinridge Long and Mrs. Long in whose loving care it has become a veritable museum of contemporary crafts.

Tulip Hill was owned by descendants of its builders, Samuel Galloway, until forty years ago. This house had its periods of neglect but was beautifully restored by Mr. and Mrs. Henry H. Flather of Washington as their summer home. It is now in the appreciative ownership of Mr. and Mrs. Lewis W. Andrews who live there the year round. It surveys West River some miles off the main highway, Md. Route 2, south of Annapolis.

Not far off U. S. Route 50 in Anne Arundel County, near the Bay Bridge, Whitehall is now close to the most up-to-date expressions of this century. But when the Ridouts sold it to Mrs. W. G. Story of Washington some fifty years ago it was a remote summer residence. Partially restored by Mrs. Story, it is now being completely reappraised by modern restoration methods under the personal supervision of the present owner, Mr. Charles Scarlett.

All that is left of Strawberry Hill are the mound and terraces on which it stood on the outskirts of West Annapolis. After Richard Sprigg returned to Cedar Park, his plantation on West River, Strawberry Hill was rented for a short time to a Belgian family. Baron Stier made it once again (1795) a show place by planting the terraces with Holland bulbs. Visitors flocked to see it in all its spring glory. But gradually the land deteriorated through neglect, so much so that Richard Parkinson, the English agriculturist, refused it as a gift. The plantation, inherited by Hugh Thompson of Baltimore who had married a Sprigg daughter, was sold off in sections until only a few acres were left around the old house. This stood until the Civil War when it was taken down to make way for a military hospital. The war ended before the hospital was finished and this building was eventually removed when the land was used for an extension of the Naval Academy.

On the Eastern Shore, in Chestertown is the Ringgold house, also known as the Abbey, or the Pearce House. It is now the home of the President of Washington College and may be visited at times. The original woodwork of the drawing room can be seen at the Baltimore Museum of Art.

The interested antiquarian may explore Buckland houses with comparative ease in Annapolis, the seat of his last and best work. A circle of some fifteen blocks on the old brick pavements of this eighteenth century town will take the visitor from house to house in less time than it takes a midshipman to traverse the twentieth century Naval Academy a few blocks in the opposite direction. A short block from the Main Gate of the Academy stand two outstanding dwellings, the Chase-Lloyd and the Hammond-Harwood houses.

Edward Lloyd, IV, the builder, died in 1796 leaving his widow to administer his large estate. His seventeen year old son eventually inherited the house and came to play an important part in the affairs of the State, becoming governor, representative in the State Legislature and United States Senator. In 1826 he sold the house, which had cost about £10,000, to his son-in-law, Henry Harwood, for $6500. At Harwood's death the house was offered for sale and was purchased by Miss Hester Ann Chase, daughter of Judge Jeremiah Townley Chase, whose residence had recently burned. Thus after seventy-five years when it had been the property of the Lloyd family, possession passed to another Chase. Miss Chase bequeathed it in 1875 to her three Chase nieces. The last surviving niece, Mrs. Hester Ann Chase Ridout, died in 1886 and left the house as a home for aged women. It is now known as The Chase Home and the first floor is open to the public.

Immediately across the street is the house now known as the Hammond-Harwood House, a period museum. Matthias Hammond never lived in his dream house because the lady of his choice jilted him. He retired to his plantation where he died in 1786, a sad end for a promising and ambitious young man. The nephew who inherited it sold it to his brother who rented it to various state officials. The James Nourse family seem to have been the first occupants, and finally Ninian Pinkney, clerk of the Executive Council, bought it in 1810 for $3,000. He soon decided that it was too large for him and sold it to Judge Jeremiah Townley Chase, a most distinguished Marylander. Judge Chase used one wing as his office and gave the house to his eldest daughter, Mrs. Richard Loockerman. It was here in 1824 that Judge Chase entertained Lafayette, conducting him through the box-lined paths of the garden, designed by Mrs. Loockerman. From her the house descended to her daughter, Mrs. William Harwood, and finally to the three unmarried Harwood daughters. When the last surviving daughter died the place was auctioned and bought in by St. John's College. In 1926 it was restored, provided with period furniture and opened to the public as a museum. The present stone steps and the iron rails at the entrance, replacing earlier wooden ones, were added at that time, but there was little structurally to do. The museum had to close during the depression and it was not until 1938 that it was again opened, this time under the auspices of a non-profit organization formed as The Hammond-Harwood House Association. As now furnished, it has the reputation of being one of the oustanding houses in America and may be seen daily for a fee.

Adjoining the Chase-Lloyd property to the northwest is that once owned by the Ogle family of Belair, two members of which, father and son, were governors of the State. Though the Ogles did not build the house, Benjamin Ogle added one of those popular semi-octagonal wings containing a ball room and made this older house more " fashionable " at the time of Buckland's residence in Annapolis. There is no documentary evidence but the woodwork might easily be from his work-shop. It was the home of old Mrs. Ogle and of the dowager Mrs. Lloyd who in 1844 advertised it for sale, describing it as having ten rooms, a spring house, a large stable and carriage house and a delightful garden enclosed by a brick wall, the " party wall " between the Lloyd and Ogle estates which is still standing. Ogle Hall was for many years the home of the Mason-Porter family but is now used as headquarters of the United States Navy Alumni Association.

Turning down Prince George Street, the visitor comes to the Paca house which is the front of Carvel Hall Hotel. The anachronistic tail wags the dog for the modern addition stretches clear through to King George Street. The old part, greatly altered, still retains the original woodwork in one room. When William Paca, a signer of the Declaration of Independence, and governor of Maryland, retired to his plantation on Wye Island on the Eastern Shore he sold his house. It changed owners many times before becoming the town's leading hotel. The inlet from the harbor which washed the foot of Paca's boasted garden has long since been filled to form part of the Naval Academy grounds.

Adjoining the Paca house is the Brice house, at the corner of Prince George and East streets. It has changed little with the years. The lot has been made much smaller and the wings have been converted into independent dwelling units but its grandeur and woodwork remain unharmed. This house had many owners through the years until it became the property of St. John's College and was divided into apartments for the faculty. It is now the home of Mr. and Mrs. Stanley Wohl who are restoring its unity and beauty.

Crossing town by way of the State Circle, one finds a visit to the State House in order. To the right of the front door is the old Senate Chamber authentically restored. About every thirty years an enterprising Legislature ordered "renovation" of its halls. During these periodic assaults on history the gallery, the desks and chairs made by John Shaw of Annapolis, and some of the woodwork disappeared. However, the state archives produced the original specifications and Trumbull, a contemporary painting of Washington's resignation, so the room is now as William Buckland planned it. Here Congress met to pass the Peace Treaty and while in session received General Washington, come to resign his commission on December 23, 1783. Thomas Mifflin of Pennsylvania in the chair, the gallery packed with ladies, veterans, congressmen and townspeople pushed to get inside to hear and see their hero. It was a highly emotional occasion. This room was used by the State senate until additions were made to the State House in 1902-5. It is now solely for exhibition purposes and open daily.

On Shipwright Street at the far end of town, stands the Scott house. The Roman Catholic Church has owned for many years all the adjoining property and a church school has encroached on old Dr. Scott's beloved garden. The house has long been the convent of the Sisters of Notre Dame who teach at the school. In this house died Sir Robert Eden in 1784 when on a business trip to Maryland and here lived the young Francis Scott Key, author of the Star-Spangled Banner, while a student at St. John's College. Though much altered in the interior it is well worth a visit. The ground floor may be seen for a small fee.

Almost on a line with the Scott house but on Duke of Gloucester Street is the Ridout house. Here again the free-standing wings have been made into separate dwellings. The main house is still lived in by a Ridout descendant. It has undergone few changes through the years but its interior glories at present in its furnishings and in the good taste and skillful restoration of its owners, Admiral and Mrs. Frederick G. Richards.

This completes the itinerary of the surviving houses attributed to William Buckland.

Appendices

INDENTURE OF APPRENTICESHIP

THIS INDENTURE WITNESSETH That William Buckland Son of Francis Buckland of the City of Oxford Yeoman—

doth put himself Apprentice to JAMES BUCKLAND Citizen and JOINER of London, to learn his Art; and with him (after the manner of an Apprentice) to serve from the Day of the Date hereof, unto the full end and term of *seven* Years, from thence next following to be fully complete and ended; During which Term, the said Apprentice his said Master faithfully shall serve, his Secrets keep, his lawful Commandments every where gladly do. He shall do no Damage to his said Master, nor see to be done of others, but that he to his Power shall let, or forthwith give warning to his said Master of the same. He shall not waste the Goods of his said Master, nor lend them unlawfully to any. He shall not commit Fornication, nor contract Matrimony within the said Term. He shall not play at Cards, Dice, Tables, or any other unlawful Games, whereby the said Master may have any Loss. With his own Goods or others, during the said Term, without Licence of his said Master, he shall neither buy nor sell. He shall not haunt Taverns, or Playhouses, nor absent himself from his said Master's Service Day nor Night unlawfully; But in all Things as a faithful Apprentice, he shall behave himself towards his said Master, and all his, during the said Term. And the said Master, (in Consideration of the Sum of   ) his said Apprentice, in the same Art which he useth, by the best Means that he can, shall teach and instruct or cause to be taught and instructed, finding unto his said Apprentice, Meat, Drink, Apparel, Lodging, and all other Necessaries, according to the Custom of the City of London, during the said Term. And for the true Performance of all and every the said Covenants and Agreements, either of the said Parties bind themselves unto the other by these Presents. In witness wheof, the Parties above-named to these Indentures interchangeably have put their Hands and Seals, the fifth Day of April in the Year of our Lord 1748 and in the Twentyfifth Year of the Reign of our Sovereign Lord George II, King of Great Britain etc

Jm Fisher Jr.   JAMES BUCKLAND

Sealed and Delivd in Presence of
Jam. Fisher

INDENTURE OF SERVICE, BUCKLAND TO MASON

THIS INDENTURE, Made the Fourth Day of August in the Twenty ninth Year of the Reign of our Sovereign Lord George Second King of Great-Britain, Etc., And in the Year of our Lord One Thousand Seven Hundred and fifty five—Between William Buckland of Oxford Carpenter & Joiner of the one Part and Thomson Mason of London Esqr.—of the other Part, Witnesseth, That the said William Buckland for the Consideration herein after-mentioned, hath, and by these Presents doth Covenant, Grant, and Agree to, and with the said Thomson Mason, his Executors and Assigns, That He the said William Buckland shall and will, as a faithful Covenant Servant, well and truly serve the said Thomson Mason, his Executors or Assigns in the Plantation of Virginia beyond the Seas, for the Space of Four Years, next ensuing his Arrival in the said Plantation, in the Employment of a Carpenter & Joiner. And the said Willm Buckland doth hereby Covenant and Declare himself, now to be the Age of Twenty two Years and Single and no Covenant or Contracted Servant to any other Person or Persons, And the said Thomson Mason for himself his Executors or Assigns, in Consideration thereof, doth hereby Covenant, Promise and Agree to and with the said Willm Buckland his Executors, and Assigns, that He the said Thomson Mason his – – – Executors or Assigns, shall and will at his or their own proper Costs and Charges, with what convenient Speed they may, carry and convey or cause to be carried and conveyed over unto the said Plantation, the said Wm Buckland and from henceforth, and during the said Voyage, and also during the said Term shall and will at the like Costs and Charges, provide for and allow the said Wm Buckland all necessary Meat, Drink, Washing, Lodging, fit and convenient for him as Covenant Servants in such Cases are usually provided for and allowed and pay and allow the said William Buckland Wages or Salary at the Rate of Twenty Pounds Sterling per Annum Payable Quarterly

And for the true Performance of the Premisses, the said Parties, to these Presents bind themselves, their Executors and Administrators, the either to the other, in the Penal Sum of Forty Pounds Sterling firmly by these Presents. IN WITNESS whereof they have hereunto interchangedly set their Hands and Seals, the Day and Year above-written.

Sealed and Delivered
   in the Presence of   Wm Buckland

Thos Hayes
Mo Kidd

THESE ARE TO CERTIFY, That the above-named Wm Buckland came before Me Gyles Lone Deputy to the Patentee at London the Day and Year above-written, and declared himself to be a single Person no Covenant or Contracted Servant to any Person or Persons; to be of the Age of Twenty-two Years; and to be desirous to serve the above-named Thomson Mason or his Assigns Four Years, according to the Tenor of the Indenture above-written. All of which is Registered in the Office for that Purpose, appointed by Letters Patents. IN WITNESS whereof, I have hereunto affixed the Common Seal of the said Office.

Gyles Lone, DPt.

[ON BACK OF INDENTURE]

4th Augt. 1755. Reced of the within named Thomson Mason Esqr.
One pound seven Shills. wch I promise to allow out of my
Wages in Virginia

W Buckland

5th August 1755 Reced. of the within named Thomson Mason Esqr. three
Pounds thirteen shillings which I promise to allow out of
my Wages in Virginia

W Buckland

*   *   *   *   *

The within named William Buckland came into Virginia with my Brother Thomson Mason who engaged him in London and had a very good Character of him there; during the time he lived with me he had the entire Direction of the Carpenters & Joiners Work of a large House; & having behaved very faithfully in my Service, I can with great Justice recommend him to any Gentleman that may have occasion to employ him, as an honest sober diligent Man, & I think a complete Master of the Carpenter's & Joiner's Business both in Theory & Practice.

G Mason

8th Novr., 1759

[Notation in Buckland's hand:]
WBuckland was born
Augt ye 14th 1734   1773
                        1734
                        ____
                        39

MORTGAGE SECURING McCALL'S LOAN TO BUCKLAND

Richmond County, Virginia, Deed Book 14, page 274.

Buckland to McCall

To ALL TO WHOME These Presents Shall Come Know ye that I—William Buckland of the Parish of Lunenburgh and County of Richmond For and in Consideration of the sum of Eighty Pounds to me in hand by Arch. McCall of the Town of Tappahannock and County of Essex Merchant At and before Sealing and Delivery of these Presents the Receipt whereof—I do hereby Acknowledge Have Given, Granted, Bargaind & Sold And by these Presents do Give, Grant, Bargain, and Sell, unto the sd. Archibald McCall The Following Horses Cattle, Hoggs, Sheep Household Goods and Chattels towit, One Grey Horse one Roan Horse, one White Horse, one Cart and one pr. Stears Twelve head of Cattle, Twelve Head of Sheep, Twelve head of Hogs Five Feather Beds & Furniture (towit Sheets, Blanketts, Quilts, Bolsters, Pillows, etc. One Desk and Book Case, One Desk Bedstead one Dressing Table One Chest of Draws, Two Dining Tables, Ten Leather Bottomd. Chairs, one Large and one Small Looking Glass Four Dozn. of Pewter plates One Dozn. Dishes one Sett of Casters Six Iron Potts one pr. of new Cart wheels one Chair and Harness TO HAVE AND TO HAVE The Abovementioned Horses, Stears, Cattle, Sheep, Hoggs, Goods & Household Furniture to Him the said Archibald McCall his heirs and Assigns to his and their only Proper use and behoof Forever Provided Neverthe less and it is the True Intent and meaning of these Presents that if I the said William Buckland do and shall well and Truly Pay or cause to be Paid unto the sd. Archibd. McCall his Exrs. Admors. or Assigns the said sum of Eighty Pounds with Legal Interest on or before the first day of April next Insuring the Date hereof then This Instrument of writing and the Sale hereof made to be void and of none Effect and I the said William Buckland for myself my heirs Exrs. and Assigns etc. do Covenant and Agree to & with the said Archibd. McCall his Exers. etc. Shall and will well and Truly Pay cause to be Paid unto the said Archibald McCall his heirs exors. etc. the said Sum of Eighty Pounds Current money with Legal Interest on the same on or before the First Day of April next Insuing the Date hereof and In Default thereof that it Shall and may be lawful for the said Archd. McCall his heirs Exors Admors etc. to Take the said horses, Stears Sheep Hoggs, Cattle, etc and Sell and Dispose therof to the best Advantage without any Lett, Suit, Trouble, or Hinderance Made or to be Made by me or any Person For me and the Amount of the Value thereof the Said Archibd. McCall his Exors Admors etc. Shall have the Licence to apply towards the Payment of the Debt aforesaid with Interest and if any Shall Remain Over and Above Sufficient to pay the same then such surplus shall be Paid and Delivered to me, my Heirs exors. etc. IN WITNESS whereof I have hereunto Set my Hand and Seal this Twenty First Day of February 1772

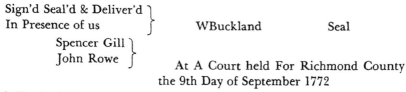

Sign'd Seal'd & Deliver'd
In Presence of us   WBuckland   Seal
        Spencer Gill
        John Rowe   At A Court held For Richmond County
                           the 9th Day of September 1772

This Deed of Mortgage From Wm Buckland of the one Part, to Archibd. McCall of the other Part, was Proved in Open Court by the Oath of Spencer Gill one of the Witness's thereto & order'd to be Lodged for Further Proof

ONE OF SEVERAL BUCKLAND ACCOUNTS IN LLOYD LEDGERS

Mr. Wm Buckland

Dr.

1773 April 26	To 1 Hatt for Mr Oliver			12	6
	To 169 feet Scantling	12/6 p. ft.	1		
	To 50 bushels Lime		1	5	
	To 3 quarts linseed Oyle			7	6
	To 1½ gallon ditto	10/per		15	
	To Cash paid on Account of M^r. McCubbin		18	18	
	To 5 days work negro Toby	3/		15	
	To 156 pound Sheet Lead		2	19	4
	To 10 Bushels Lime	6d.		5	
	To Cash paid this day in full of Workman's Wages		32	5	
	To Cash paid Travis Garland p. his . . .		6		
	To Ballance due Wm Buckland per Contra		222	2	
			£287	4	4

INVENTORY OF ESTATE

An Inventory of the Goods and Chattels of William Buckland late of Ann Arundel County deceased—Appraised in Current Money of this Province by us the Subscribers (being thereto legally authorized and sworn this 19th December Anno Domini 1774—

Thomas Waits a Man Servant and Bricklayer	£ 20– –
John Trutton ditto ditto	20– –
Samuel Baily a Carpenter and Joiner	16– –
Michael Burke a Painter	10– –
James Reynolds a Carver	16– –
Lawrence Ohern	2–10–
Oxford a Negroe Man	60– –
Sue a Negroe Woman	25– –
Hannah a Young Negroe Woman	50– –
Joe a Negroe Boy	15– –
Beck a Negroe Girl	12– –
3 Chests Carpenters Tools	15– –
One Chest Carvers ditto	1– –
Two cows	5– –
One Mahogany Desk & BookCase	12– –
One ditto Dining Table	2– 8–
One ditto Tea ditto	1– 4–
One Walnut Chest of Drawers	2– –
One Walnut Dining Table	1– 4–
One ditto sideBoard	–16–
Six Mahogany Chairs	3– –
One Bed Bedstead and Furniture	6– –
One ditto	5– –
One ditto	6– –
One ditto	6
One ditto	2– 8–
One Mattrass	–16–
Three Arm Chairs	– 4–
One Black Walnutt Chest	– 6–
One Pine ditto	– 4–

One Gin Case & Bottles	–15–
One small Black Walnutt Chest	–10–
One Mahogany Tea ditto	–10–
One Spinning Wheel	–10–
A Parcel of Earthen Ware	5– –
A parcel of Glass ditto	–10–
One pair Hand Irons with Tongs Shovel & Poker	1– 5–
One pair ditto with ditto	–16–
Two Box Irons and Heaters & three flatt Irons	–12–
One pine Case and Nine Bottles	– 6–
One Warming Pane	–12–
Two Tea Kettles and Coffee Pott	–12–
Four Chafing Dishes	–10–
109 lb Pewter 10ᵈ	4–10–10
4 Brass Candlesticks	– 8–
1 small Pine Chest and one large	– 4– 6
1 Stew Pan & Skillett	– 6–
1 Dripping Pan and Spit	– 5–
1 Frying Pan Ladle fflesh fork and Skimmer	– 4–
2 Squares and Bevils and two Drawing Boards	– 6–
1 Lanthorn and pair Bellows	– 4–
1 Table Castor	–10–
2 Scrubbing Brushes	– 2– 6
A quantity of Wooden Ware in the Kitchen	– 4–
One Griddle and Grid Iron	– 2– 6
Two Iron pot Racks and Hooks, Hand Irons etc	–12–
One Whip Saw and one x cut Saw	1– –
One Silver Watch	4–10–
One large looking Glass	2– –
One Small ditto	– 8–
One Servants Bed with Sheets & Blanketts	1– 8–
Two Old Mattrasses with Blanketts etc.	1– –
Two Well Bucketts	–12–
One Tin Waterer for the Gardens	– 6–
One Case of Razor Strap & Hone	– 4–
One Trunk 1/ 6 Napkins 6/ 4 TableCloths 6/	–13–
One Bed Tick Bolster and Pillow Cases	1–16–
Five Counterpains	5– –
7 prs. Course Old Sheets	2–10–
1 Cradle with Bed Cloths	–12–

6 pr fall Shoes		1–16–
A parcel of Bottles Jugs etc		– 8–
6 Oil Juggs		– 3–
10 Knives and Forks		– 6–
A parcel of Old Lumber		– 8–
One Iron Coffee Mill		– 8–
One Marble Ink Stand		– 3–
One Calf Skin		– 5–
Old Lumber consisting of Carpenters old Tools etc		1– –
One Hone		– 1– 4
4 Trowels 1 Lath & Hammer & 2 old Spades		– 4–
77 Squares of Glass in box 11 by 9	a 8^d	2–11– 4
19 doz quart Bottles		1–18–
5 doz pint Bottles	1/per doz	– 5–
33 Chestnut posts for pailing		1– 2–
45 three Square railed Rails	at 10/pr hund.	– 4– 6
491 Cleft ditto	at 18/pr do	4– 8– 4½
537 Cleft pail Boards	at 20/pr thod.	–11– 1½
12 Oz 13 Cwt. Silver Plate	@ 6/9	4– 5– 4½
136 lb Pot Iron	3^d	1–14–
46 lb Glue	1/	2– 6–
630 feet of 1½ Inch pine Plank	@ 8/pr h.	2–10– 4¾
960 feet of Old plank uppon the Scaffolds & lying in and about the Building	4/	1–18– 4¾
400 feet of Old pine Scantling laying abt. the Lotts and Building much damaged	6/	1– 4–
30 Bushs Hair	16^d	2– –
Cash in the House		2– 4–
A Parcel of drawing paper		–16–
A Case of Mathematical Instruments		2– –
5 Vols of the Fool of Quality [by Henry Brooke, 1706-1783]		–12–
8 Vols Turkish Spy [*Letters Written by a Turkish Spy*, London, 1741]		1–10–
Wares Designs [Isaac Ware, *A Complete Body of Architecture*, London, 1756]		2– –
Gibbs Designs [James Gibbs, *A Book of Architecture*, London, 1728]		2– –
Swans British Treasuary [Abraham Swan, *British Treasury*, London, 1745]		– 8–
Swans Architect [A. Swan, *British Architect*, London, 1745]		–12–

The London Art [*of Building*, by William Salmon, London, 1748]	– 1–
Langleys Designs [Batty Langley, *The City & Country Builder's and Workman's Treasury of Designs*, London, 1756]	–10–
Chippendales Designs [*The Gentleman's & Cabinet Makers' Guide*, London, 1754]	– 6–
Kirbys Prospective 2 vols [John Joshua Kirby, *Methods of Perspective Made Easy*, Ipswich, 1754]	1– –
Lightholders Designs [Thomas Lightholder, *The Gentleman & Farmers' Architect*, London, 1762]	– 8–
Langleys Gothic Architecture [Batty Langley, London, 1747]	– 6–
Essay on ditto	– 4–
Tillotsons *Sermons* 3 Vols. [Archbishop John Tillotson, London, 1695]	–16–
Johnsons Carver's Designs [Thomas Johnson, Carver, *150 New Designs*, London, 1761]	– 2–
Hoppuss' Measurer [Edward Hoppus, *The Gentleman's & Builder's Repository or Architecture Displayed*, London, 1761]	– 1–
Factors Guide	– 1–
Reeds Reckoner [Reid]	– 1–
Swans Carpenters Instruction [A. Swan, *Designs in Carpentry*, London, 1759]	– 4–
Morris's Designs [Robert Morris, *Select Architecture*, London, 1757]	– 1–
Old Magazines etc.	–12–
Wearing Apparel	12– –
180 lb. 4d Nails	2– 8–10
320 lb. 3d ditto	6–12–
450 lb 10d ditto	9– 1–4
3500 Bricks	3–10–
60 Bushl. Lime	1– –
2 Ornamented Ceilings of Paper	10– –
1 large white Picture frame	2– –
2 ditto blacked	1– –
5 Table frames @ 4/ Each	1– –
1 Quilting frame	– 4–
2 Work Benches at 5/	–10–
2 Ladders 5/ 2 Pannelled Doors 16/6	1–16–6
3 Battened Doors	–12–

1 Homney Mortor 5/		– 5–
1 Large Jar & a Qty of Soap		– 8–
73 lb. Hoggs Fatt & Jars containing the same 4d		1– 4–4
12 Books Gold Leaf & Damaged		– 6–
1 Spice Mortar & Pestle		– 3–
Old Kns. & forks		– 1–
Butlers Annalogy [Joseph Butler, Bishop of Durham, *The Analogy of Religion*, London, 1736.]		– 1–
1 Small Picture frame part[?] finished		– 3–
2 Lotts of Ground with the Houses and Improvements thereon		200– –
2 Iron Grates wt 96 lb	4	1–12–
124 Sash Lights 10 by 8	6	3– 2–
225 ditto 14 by 12	6	5–12–6
1 Stock Mahogany 10 feet	11	–10–

£672–11–8

J Duckett ⎫
Joshua Frazier ⎬apprs

Sarah Buckland ⎫
Francis Buckland ⎬Kin

James Williams ⎫
Lanct. Jacques ⎬Creditors

Prerogative Office to Wit Came Denton Jac-
    June 3ᵈ 1777—   ques and John Ran-
dal and as admrs of Wᵐ Buckland late of Ann
Arundel Coty made Oath that this is a Just and
true Inventory of the Goods and Chattels of the
deceased that have come to their hands or possession at the time of making the Same, and that
what shall hereafter come to their hands they
will return in an additional Inventory that they
do not know of any concealment of the deceased's Estate, and that if they shall hereafter
discover any concealments they will acquaint
the Commissary with it that it may be inquired
into according to Law

Sworn to before me

Elie Vallette Reg.ᵗ

FINAL ACCOUNT OF ESTATE

The account of Mary Buckland, Denton Jacques and John Randall admsrs. of William Buckland late of Anne Arundel County deceased THESE ACCOUNTANTS Charge themselves with the amount of the deceased Inventory herewith Exhibited of...................... £672–11–8

By sundry Effects Since come to hand and Sold as flows Vizt—

3 Vols of Dictionairies of Arts and Sciences	5– 5–0	
22 of Oyl 4/3 Bushels of Hair 6/4th Whiting	2/0–12–8	5– 3– 6
25 Bushels of Lime	–12–6	

Received from Mr. Brice for work done to the Time of Sale deducting for board and maintenance of the Servant   2–10–0

By so much gained on finishing Mr. Hammonds House   96–17–6

Also for the following Debts received Vizt
From William Waller   31– 5–0

From Bennet Chew   2– 1–0

From Charles Roberts   3– 0–0

£105–10–6% per 108–10– 9½

And they Crave to be allowed for the following   £786– 5–11½
Payments Vizt.—

Of Common money paid to Commissary General & deputy for Letters of admin.   2–11– 9

Of Do. money paid to Isaac Greentree for his Expenses for the funeral of the deceased   10– 0– 0

Of do. money due from the deceased to James Buchanan and Company on his Bond dated 6th July 1774 for 79 £ 11–5 and paid by these Accountants with Interest thereon, as per said Bond proved and receipt appears   80– 0–11

By Do. money due from the deceased to Richard Maccubbin and paid by these Accountants as per Judgment rendered and receipt thereon appears   9– 4– 0

On 75 £ Sterling money due from the deceased to the Loan Office on his Bond dated the 10 August 1774 and paid by these Account's with Interest thereon to November 1775 as per said Bond proved and receipt appears 78 £ 12–6 at 66⅔   131– 0–10

Of Common money due from the deceased to William Hardy on his Bond, and paid by these Accountants as per Bond proved and receipt thereon appears   40– 4– 7

Of Do. money due from Do. to Robert Couden, and paid by these Accountants as per Judgement rendered and receipt thereon apprs.   16– 2– 6

Of Do. money secured to be paid by these Accountants for appraising the Estate 2 Days   2– 0– 0

Of 296–18–1 Common money due from the deceased on his mortgage to James Williams and paid by these Accountants with charge of deed and Interest thereon till December 1775 as per said Mortgage and receipt appears   322– 3– 1

Of Common money paid for recording the Inventory   –12– 6

Of Do. money paid for recording this Account   0– 8– 6

Of Do. money paid for Stating & Drawing this Account   1–15– 0

Of Ten per Cent Commission allowed on paying the above sum   61–12– 4

£677–16– 0

Deduct ⅕ to reduce it to Current Money   135–11– 2½

£542– 4– 9½

Balance due to the Estate in the hands
of the Adminsts.   244– 1– 2
                                                               ─────────
                                                               £786– 5–11½

Time prayed to pass on additional account
A List of Debts Desperate will be returned hereafter
Perogative Offce   Came Denton Jacques and John Randall
   June 3 1777   the within Accountants and made Oath
                        that the Account is Just and true as
                        Stated which thereupon is passed by
                        order of William Fitzhugh Comr. Genl.
                        Test   Elie Vallette Regt.

Notes to the Text

NOTES, CHAPTER I, Pages 1 to 11.

Background for this chapter: Sir Walter Besant, *London in the Eighteenth Century* (London, 1902); T. F. Reddaway, *The Rebuilding of London after the Great Fire* (London, 1940); John Summerson, *Architecture in Britain, 1530 to 1830* (Penguin Books, Baltimore, 1954); Nikolaus Pevsner, *London,* (The Buildings of England) (London, 1952).

1. Baptized Sept. 8, 1734, Transcripts of Oxford Parish Records, Manuscript Room Bodleian Library, Oxford University. Birth recorded by William Buckland on back of his contract with Mason (Appendix B), owned by Mr. Richard H. Randall of Baltimore.

2. Records of the Joiners' Company, Guild Hall Library, London, MS 8052/6; also indenture of apprenticeship, William Buckland to James Buckland, owned by Mr. Randall. (Appendix A).

3. Records of Joiners' Company.

4. *Ibid.*

5. Evans Austin, ed., *The Law Relating to Apprentices* (London, 1890).

6. Records of the Joiners' Company. For many years James Buckland, the joiner of London and the uncle of William, was thought to be James Buckland, 1711-1790, bookseller and publisher "At the Sign of the Buck," corner of St. Paul's Court and Paternoster Row. The late R. T. H. Halsey in his preface to *Great Georgian Houses of America* (New York, 1933), makes such an assertion. It is recorded that the latter was a "bookseller of eminence," a "remarkably gentlemanly-looking personage in the (oldfashioned) dress of George II's days" and a man of substance. In his will (at Somerset House) he calls himself "Bookseller and Carpenter," not Joiner. Because of ancient rivalry between the Carpenters' and Joiners' Companies it is most unlikely that anyone was a member of both. This James was a very different person from the humble joiner of Dean St., Holborn, the uncle of William, who is known only through the entries in the books of the Company of Joiners.

7. Records of Joiners' Company.

8. Indenture between Buckland and Mason, Aug. 4, 1755. See note 1.

9. *Ibid.*

NOTES, CHAPTER II, Pages 12 to 21.

Background material: Rev. Andrew Burnaby, *Travels through the Middle Settlements in North-America in the Years 1759 and 1760* (London, 1775); "Diary of John Harrower 1773-1776," in the *American Historical Review,* VI (1901), 65-107; Port of Entry Papers, Maryland Historical Society; "Journal of a French Traveller in the American Colonies," *American Historical Review,* XXVI (1921), 726-747; XXVII (1921) 70-89; Abbott E. Smith, *Colonists in Bondage* (Chapel Hill, N. C., 1947); Newton D. Mereness, *Maryland as a Proprietary Province* (New York, 1901); John W. Tebbel, *George Washington's America* (New York, 1954).

1. Indenture, Buckland to Mason.
2. William W. Hening, *Statutes at Large* ... *of Virginia* (Richmond, 1819), VI, 498.
3. Kate Mason Rowland, *Life of George Mason* (New York, 1892), I, 48.
4. Thomas J. Wertenbaker, *Patrician and Plebian in Virginia* (Charlottesville, 1910), and *Planters of Colonial Virginia* (Princeton, 1922); Carl Bridenbaugh, *Seat of Empire* (Williamsburg, [1950].
5. A. E. Smith, *op. cit.*, p. 336.
6. *Letters and Recollections of George Washington; Being Letters to Tobias Lear and Others between 1790 and 1799* (New York, 1906), p. 120.
7. Lafayette, *Mémoires, correspondance et manuscrits du général La Fayette*, ed. by F. de Corcelle (Paris, 1837-1838) I, 93-94.
8. "With Braddock's Army" (Diary of Mrs. Browne), *Virginia Magazine of History*, XXXII (1924), 311-320.
9. Rowland, I, 1-58; Helen Day Hill, *George Mason, Constitutionalist* (Cambridge, Mass., 1938).
10. Charles W. Stetson, *Washington and His Neighbors* (Richmond, [1956]).

NOTES, CHAPTER III, Pages 22 to 33.

1. Rowland, I, 57.
2. *Notes on the State of Virginia* (Boston, 1801), p. 225-227.
3. Note on back of Buckland-Mason indenture.
4. Marietta Minnigerode Andrews, *George Washington's Country* (New York, [1930]), p. 54-56. Mason to Alexander Henderson, July 18, 1763.
5. General John Mason of Analostan Island, quoted in Rowland, I, 99-101.
6. Dr. Alexander Hamilton's "Itinerarium" of 1744, edited by Carl Bridenbaugh as *Gentleman's Progress* (Chapel Hill, 1948).
7. *The Journal of Nicholas Cresswell, 1774-1777* (New York, 1924); Philip Vickers Fithian, *Journal and Letters, 1767-1774* (Princeton, 1900); John Davis, *Travels of Four Years and a Half in the United States of America* (London, 1803).
8. Business ledgers of John Glassford & Co. of Colchester, Library of Congress. "1758: Account with Geo. Mason, Esq., for Wm. Buckland 3 prs worsted stockings, 2 hammers, thread, metal buttons, Buckram, oznig, hair." Sept. 1758 to 1760, William Buckland's personal account: "1 gal Rum, sugar, 1 gal Brandy, Ribbon [3 times], cambric, linen, striped holland, pumps, buckles, lawn handkerchief, Bridle, pumps for J. McAlley, necklace, knitting needles, total £4:2:1 paid."
9. Davis, p. 244. Davis was tutor to the Ellicott family at Occoquan.
10. Fairfax County Deeds, Liber B, f. 103: Liber G, f. 275; Liber C 1, f. 248.
11. Philip Slaughter, *History of Truro Parish* (Philadelphia, 1908), p. 18-20, quotes vestry book for Aug. 8, 1743.
12. Fairfax County Wills, Liber 1, f. 66, probated Oct. 16, 1769. Fairfax County Wills (Mary Moore) Liber C 1, f. 248; and Inventory, C 1, f. 92, 93. It is possible that Moore was a builder as well as a planter. One of the same name

was "undertaker" of "the new church at Redman's," 1755-1757, Dettingen Parish Vestry book. This was near the Moore farms.

13. Endorsement on back of Buckland-Mason indenture.

14. Prayer Book owned by Mr. Charles Harrison Mann of Jacksonville, Florida.

15. Glassford accounts.

16. Slaughter, p. 34, and an advertisement in *The Virginia Gazette* for March 5, 1767, giving a complete description of the glebe house.

17. Research of late owner, Mr. F. A. Barnes. *Virginia, A Guide to the Old Dominion,* American Guide Series (New York, 1940), p. 344.

18. Buckland—Brent suit, Richmond County Order Book 15, 1763. See Ch. IV.

19. Fairfax County Deeds, Liber C 1, f. 806. Also Harrison Williams, *Legends of Loudoun* (Richmond, 1938), p. 77, and Fairfax Harrison, *Landmarks of Old Prince William* (Richmond, 1924) for background.

20. Robert A. Lancaster, *Historic Virginia Houses and Churches* (Philadelphia, 1915), has the photograph and date, p. 378.

NOTES, CHAPTER IV, Page 34 to 48.

1. For John Ariss, ca. 1725-1799, see Thomas Tileston Waterman, *The Mansions of Virginia, 1706-1776* (Chapel Hill, 1945). Following publication, Mr. Waterman changed his attribution of Menokin, Blandfield and Elmwood from Ariss to Buckland when through one of the authors he learned of the latter's presence in the Northern Neck. New material is found in Richmond County Deeds 12, f. 344, 355 and Order Book 14, f. 438. Also "List of Rentals due the President of the United States, Berkeley County, Va. Tenants for Dec. 25, 1792, John Ariss £60:0:0," manuscript collection, the Mount Vernon Ladies' Association of the Union.

2. Daniel French, 1723-1771, had built the "gaol and stocks for Loudoun County" in 1758-1761 and was the original contractor for Pohick Church in 1769. He rented the estate which Ariss afterwards bought. Richmond County Deeds 12, f. 344, 1762.

3. Richmond County Order Book 15, f. 293.

4. Waterman, *op. cit.,* p. 260.

5. Sabine Hall Collection, Alderman Library, University of Virginia, Charlottesville.

6. Richmond County Order Book 15, July 6, 1763; Carter Papers, Folder 2, William & Mary College Library, Williamsburg, Va.

7. Richmond County Order Book 15, July 1763-1764, f. 293.

8. Richmond County Order Books 14, 15, 16.

9. Richmond County Deeds 12, Oct. 3, 1765; Feb. 2, Aug. 3, Oct. 6, Dec. 7, 1767.

10. Richmond County Order Book 15, f. 293: "Sheriff pay the money in his hands to wit seven pounds, twelve shillings and five pence to Wm. Buckland towards paying for building the prison."

11. Diary of Robert Wormeley Carter for 1766-1768, Carter Papers, William & Mary College Library. Also Richmond County Order Books 15, f. 293, and 16, f. 190; Hening, VIII, 204.

12. See the Rev. Jonathan Boucher, *Reminiscences of an American Loyalist* (Boston & New York, 1925), p. 30 *passim*, and Warren Hunting Smith, *Originals Abroad* (New Haven, 1952), p. 79-93.

13. Sabine Hall Collection.

14. Carter Papers.

15. *Ibid.*

16. Beverley Letter Book, Manuscript Div., Library of Congress.

17. Richmond County Order Book 15, 1764, " Grandjury vs. Wm. Buckland."

18. Richmond County Order Book 16, f. 410.

19. *Ibid.*, f. 201.

20. *Ibid.*, f. 426. The Callises were witnesses in the Brent-Buckland suit where the item of £8:10:0 for a silver watch appears.

21. Richmond County Order Book 16, Sept. 9, 1772.

22. Anne Arundel County, Md., Inventories, Liber 125, f. 337, Hall of Records, Annapolis.

23. William Buckland to Hon. Robert Carter, Keith-Carter Collection, Virginia Historical Society, Richmond.

24. *Ibid.*

25. Fithian, *op. cit.*, p. 100.

26. Lloyd business ledgers, MdHS.

27. Fithian, *op. cit.*, p. 152-154.

28. Richmond County Deeds 14, f. 274, 275.

29. See note 21.

Notes, Chapter V, Page 67 to 81.

Travellers have left many records of Maryland, and Annapolis in particular, at this period in its history. The most valuable are the *Journal of a French Traveller in the American Colonies*, already cited; Lord Adam Gordon, " Journal of an Officer's Travels in America and the West Indies, 1764-1765," in *Travels in the American Colonies, 1764-1765*, ed. by Newton D. Mereness (New York, 1916) ; Abbé Robin, *New Travels through North America* (Boston, 1784). Indispensible are the Rev. Jonathan Boucher, *Reminiscences*, and William Eddis, *Letters from America* (London, 1792). Mereness, *Maryland as a Proprietary Province* (New York, 1901), and Arthur M. Schlesinger, *The Colonial Merchants and the American Revolution, 1763-1776* (New York, 1918), are helpful as background.

1. Port of Entry Papers, Maryland Hist. Soc. (hereafter Md. HS) .

2. Nicholson was Royal Governor of New York, Virginia, Nova Scotia and North Carolina, and of Maryland, 1694-1699.

3. 1718 map by James Stoddert. Later copy in Land Office, Annapolis.

4. Elbridge Gerry to Stephen Higginson, March 4, 1784, Edmund C. Burnett, ed., *Letters of Members of the Continental Congress* (Washington, 1934) and

[Edward Kimber], "Itinerant Observations in America [1745]" *Md. Hist. Mag.*, LI (1956), 336.

5. Thomas Eden, the only brother not to acquire a title, was in trade between London and Maryland. He later became Deputy Auditor of Greenwich Hospital, England. Colonel William Fitzhugh, 1725-1791, was a Virginian who married the Widow Rousby of Calvert County, Md., and lived at Rousby Hall. Commissioned in the British army, member of the Council of both Sharpe and Eden, he sympathized with the colonists and as reward had his house burned by the British fleet. He later was elected to the Council of State in 1776 and to the Maryland Constitutional Convention.

6. Primrose Hill on Spa Creek was bought by Richard Young before 1748. His daughter married the artist John Hesselius so the place became known as the Hesselius place. Acton built by Philip Hammond, older brother of Matthias, is also on Spa Creek. Belvoir on the south bank of the Severn River was built by John Ross. His two daughters, Mrs. Upton Scott and Mrs. Henry Maynadier, shared the plantation almost until 1800. Stepney, below South River, was the home of Daniel of St. Thomas Jenifer when, in 1775 the Council met there to tell Governor Eden it was best for him to leave the colony. Whitehall, the seat of Governor Horatio Sharpe has been dealt with most thoroughly by the present owner, Charles Scarlett, Jr., *Md. Hist. Mag.*, XLVI (1951), 8-26.

7. Minutes of the Homony Club, Gilmor Papers, MdHS. Fuller minutes are in the Historical Society of Pennsylvania, Philadelphia.

8. Eddis, *passim*, and Mrs. Rebecca Key, "A Notice of Some of the First Buildings," *Md. Hist. Mag.*, XIV (1919), 258-271.

9. John Carter Brown Library, Providence, R. I.

10. Eddis, 17-20.

11. See Katharine Scarborough, *Homes of the Cavaliers* (New York, 1930); David Ridgely, *Annals of Annapolis* (Baltimore, 1841); Walter B. Norris, *Annapolis, Its Colonial and Naval History* (New York), [1925]).

12. Daniel Dulany to Robert Carter, Oct. 22, 1764, Carter Papers, Folder 18, William & Mary College Library. Charles Carroll of Carrollton's letter to Daniel Barrington, Dec. 22, 1765, *Unpublished Letters of Charles Carroll of Carrollton*, compiled and edited by Thomas M. Field (New York, 1902).

13. Upton Scott to his father Francis Scott of Temple Patrick, Co. Antrim, Ireland, Dec. 30, 1765, owned by the Misses Annan, Taneytown, Md.

14. Scarlett, *op. cit.*; *Archives of Md.*, XIV, 550; Anne Arundel Co. Wills, 1797, Hall of Records; Lady Edgar, *A Colonial Governor in Maryland* (London, 1912).

15. Charles Willson Peale, "Autobiography," American Philosophical Society, Philadelphia; entry for June 29, 1824.

16. Joshua Johnson to Charles Wallace, Dec. 1, 1771, Wallace, Davidson & Johnson Letter Book, Hall of Records.

17. Watercolor owned by Mrs. W. D. Nelson Thomas of Baltimore; "Calvert-Stier Correspondence," *Md. Hist. Mag.*, XXXVIII (1943) 128; Diary of William Faris, April 27, 1797, MdHS; Richard Parkinson, *A Tour in America* (London, 1805), II, 65; Memoirs of Richard Sprigg Steuart, 1868, unpublished MS, copy at MdHS; Tax Assessment List, 1798, Anne Arundel County, MdHS.

18. *Diaries of George Washington*, ed. by John C. Fitzpatrick (Boston, 1925), entry for Sept. 29, 1773.

19. Francis B. Culver, *Blooded Horses of Colonial Days* (Baltimore, 1922), 47, 52.

20. Washington, *Diaries*, Sept. 22, 1771.

21. Research of J. Reaney Kelly. L. M. Leisenring, "Tulip Hill, Anne Arundel Co.," *Md. Hist. Mag.*, XLVII (1952), 188-208.

22. Kent County Wills, Liber 38, f. 624; Testamentary Proceedings, Liber 44, f. 374, 1771-2, Hall of Records.

23. *Archives of Md.*, XIV, 412, 421.

24. *Kent News*, Chestertown, Md., n. d., courtesy of Mr. L. Wethered Barroll; Galloway Papers, Library of Congress; Raymond B. Clark, Jr., "The Abbey, or Ringgold House," *Md. Hist. Mag.*, XLVI (1951), 81-92.

25. *News-Record* of the Baltimore Museum of Art, Vol. 4, No. 6 (1932).

NOTES, CHAPTER VI, Pages 82 to 102.

1. Faris Day Book, MdHS. For Faris' life see J. Hall Pleasants and Howard Sill, *Maryland Silversmiths, 1715-1830* (Baltimore, 1930); Lockwood Barr, "William Faris, 1728-1804," *Md. Hist. Mag.*, XXXVI (1941), 420-439.

2. Mayor's Court Records, Annapolis, Vol. 3, 1766-1772, Hall of Records.

3. Edward Lloyd, III, 1711-1770, Anne Arundel County Wills, J. G. 2 (37) f. 469, Hall of Records. Edward Lloyd, IV, 1744-1796, elected for Talbot Co. 1771.

4. Provincial Court Deeds, D. D. 5, f. 259, Land Office, Annapolis. J. Donnell Tilghman, "Bill for the Construction of the Chase House," *Md. Hist. Mag.*, XXXIII (1938), 23-26.

5. R. R. Beirne, "The Chase House in Annapolis," *Md. Hist. Mag.*, XLIX (1954), 177-196.

6. Lloyd ledger. The servant man at Middleton's Hotel was paid "6 shillings 3 pence for his beating the Drum Tunes round Town."

7. See poem by Rev. Jonathan Boucher in the *Maryland Gazette*, Sept. 5, 1771.

8. Lloyd ledger, September 26, 1771. Buckland bought "sundries to the value of £ 7;14;8½ "

9. Washington, *Diaries*, Sept. 24, 1771.

10. Culver, *op. cit.*, p. 63.

11. *The Maryland Gazette*, Sept., 1771, advertisement of the New American Company (Hallam-Douglass) and its repertoire.

12. Tilghman, *op. cit.*

13. Randall family records. These are also authority for details of John Randall's early career. Comparative salaries in those days: Buckland paid James Brent £10 per annum; Fithian, a tutor, received £40 and Edward Lloyd's gardener £30:10.0.

14. Tilghman, *op. cit.*

15. Jonathan Boucher to George Washington, Feb. 21, 1772; Stanislaus M. Hamilton, ed., *Letters to Washington* (Boston, 1901), IV, 109.

16. Anne Arundel County Deeds, 4 IB., f. 529, 530, Aug. 15, 1772. These lots were near the site of the B. & A. Station.

17. Charles Carroll to his son, Charles Carroll of Carrollton, II, 32, April 10, 1770, and III, 15, Oct. 19, 1772, Carroll Papers, MdHS.

18. Richmond County, Va., Deeds, 14, f. 275, previously cited.

19. Faris Day Book.

20. *Maryland Gazette*, July 22, 1773.

21. Eddis, p. 138.

22. "Calvert-Stier Correspondence," *Md. Hist. Mag.*, XXXVIII (1943), 128.

23. John Brice's will, Anne Arundel County Wills, 1766; H. F. Sturdy and A. Trader, *Seeing Annapolis* (Baltimore, 1949), p. 19.

24. *Maryland Gazette* March 4, 1773. There is indication in the letter books of Wallace, Davidson and Johnson, that James Brice was in 1773 about to marry. 1773, Sept., London: "Am a little surprised to hear that Lloyd Dulany had married B. Brice [Elizabeth sister of James, married June 15, 1773] but much more so to hear that James had married Miss Skinner[.] 1600 to[o] little for matrimony."

25. Anne Arundel County Judgments D. G. 1, f. 230, 482, 1772-1773.

26. Anne Arundel County Deeds 4 IB, f. 529, 1772-1774.

27. Eddis, p. 128.

28. *Maryland Gazette*, October 21, 1773.

29. *Ibid.*, December 16, 1773, to February 17, 1774.

30. *Maryland Journal & Baltimore Advertiser*, November 27 to December 30, 1773.

31. Benjamin Ogle, 1746-1809, son of Gov. Samuel Ogle of Belair married his second wife, Henrietta Maria Hill, in 1770. He was elected governor 1798. Lloyd Dulany, 1742-1782, brother of Daniel Dulany the Younger, was educated in England, married Elizabeth Brice, but retired at the outbreak of the Revolution to England where he was killed in a duel by the Rev. Bennet Allen as the result of a family feud begun in Maryland. His house on Conduit St. is of all-header bond and is said to have cost £10,000. Elizabeth Bordley, daughter of Thomas Bordley who built the house off the "Public Circle" before 1732, was the sister of two prominent lawyers, Stephen and John Beale Bordley, both members of the Governor's Council. Governor Eden's mansion was built prior to 1750 by Edmund Jenings, Secretary of the Colony. It stood on the site of the present Bancroft Hall in the Naval Academy grounds. Robert Key was employed to enlarge it in 1768. The Ball or Assembly Room on Duke of Gloucester St. was built after 1765 (see advertisement in the *Gazette*, May 23, 1765) while the new theatre, replacing an earlier one, opened Oct., 1771 (Eddis, p. 108).

32. *Maryland Gazette*, April 2, 1772.

33. Morris L. Radoff, *Buildings of the State of Maryland* (Annapolis, 1954), p. 85; MS Memorial of Charles Wallace to the Assembly, Dec. 20, 1779, Hall of Records; Wallace, Davidson and Johnson Letter Book, March 24, and May 17, 1774.

34. *Maryland Gazette*, April 2, 1772.

35. *Votes and Proceedings of the House of Delegates*, Nov. Session, 1779, p. 73, 78.

36. *Archives of Maryland*, LXIV, 143.

37. Randall family records. For 1904 restoration see *The Maryland State House: Memorial to J. Appleton Wilson* (Baltimore, Society of Colonial Wars, [1931?]).

38. The Commissioners of the Loan Office to Wm. Buckland, March 22, 1774, Scharf Papers, MdHS.

NOTES, CHAPTER VII, pages 103 to 114.

1. Slaughter, p. 81. "The Church Wardens are directed to agree with persons to make such carved ornaments on the altarpiece as they shall judge proper." Specifications for building the church are in Martin Cockburn's business ledger, 1767-1773, 1765-1818, Library of Congress, as well as in the Vestry Minutes. Cockburn, Mason's most intimate friend, was a vestryman of Truro Parish.

2. Bishop William Meade, *Old Churches and Families of Virginia* (Philadelphia, 1857), II, 226.

3. Minutes of the Forensic Club, 1759-1767, MdHS.

4. Faris Day Book.

5. *Maryland Gazette*, April 3-28, 1774.

6. *Ibid.*, June 13-Sept. 8, 1774.

7. *Ibid.*, May 25, 1774.

8. *Ibid.*, May 30, 1774. Also see Eddis, p. 159-166.

9. *Maryland Gazette*, Aug. 16, 1764. For background see Charles A. Barker, *Background of the Revolution in Maryland* (New Haven, 1940); J. Thomas Scharf, *History of Maryland*, Vol. II (Baltimore, 1879); *Journal of a French Traveller*, and Eddis, *op. cit.*

10. Peale Diary, cited by Charles Coleman Sellers, *Portraits and Miniatures by Charles Willson Peale* (Philadelphia, 1952). John Callahan, 1749-1803, Register of the Land Office and owner of a charming small house which stood at the corner of College Ave. and Bladen St., now moved and known as "the Pinkney House," married Sarah Buckland, William's daughter. Callahan was a cousin of Peale's, a vestryman of St. Anne's Church and a lieutenant in the Continental forces. Peale later painted portraits of John, Sarah with her youngest daughter, and one of the two other little girls. All four of these portraits were inherited by the Misses Harwood, the great great granddaughters of William Buckland and all but his still hang in the Hammond-Harwood House, Annapolis. Buckland's portrait is in the Mabel Brady Garvan Collection at Yale University.

11. *Maryland Gazette*, Aug. 6, 1772, July 1, 1773, July 14, 1774.

12. Anne Arundel County Deeds 4 IB, 1773-1774, f. 529, 530. Mortgage executed Aug. 11, 1774.

13. *Laws of Maryland*, Chapter XI, 1774.

14. *Maryland Gazette*, October 20, 27, Nov. 3, 1774; Eddis, p. 171-184; Galloway letter, Hist. Soc. of Penna.; Loyalist Records from the British Archives, Fisher Papers, MdHS.

15. Wallace, Davidson & Johnson Letter Book.
16. Eddis, p. 187, 210.
17. *Maryland Gazette*, Nov. 8, 1774, State Library, Annapolis.
18. *Archives of Maryland*, LXIV, 211-212, Nov. 1773.
19. Newspaper photograph, Denton, Md., n. d., in possession of R. R. Beirne.
20. Fithian, *op. cit.*, p. 105-106.
21. "Isaac Greentree for funeral—£10.0," Anne Arundel County Accounts, Liber 72, f. 421, 1775. Greentree appears in Talbot and Queen Anne's counties as tavern and ferry keeper, and Assistant Commissary. Elie Vallette, *The Deputy Commissary's Guide* (Annapolis, 1774), p. 39, "Allowance for funeral not to exceed 3 or 4 pounds except where rank and opulence may require."
22. Anne Arundel County Testamentary Proceedings, Liber 46, f. 108; 83, f. 41, Dec. 1774.
23. *Maryland Gazette*, Dec. 15, 1774.
24. *Ibid.*, May 9, 1775.
25. Anne Arundel County Deeds, 5 IB, f. 367, Dec. 18, 1776, and Chancery Court Records, B, f. 133-422, Sept. term, 1826.
26. Mary Buckland died in Annapolis, *Maryland Gazette*, Aug. 10, 1810, and Mann Prayer Book. For Sarah Callahan see Note 10. It has previously been stated that the widow, Mary Buckland, married George Mann, 1752-1794, on June 30, 1779 (Index of Md. Marriages, Hall of Records). It now seems certain that this Mary Buckland was William's daughter, Mary Moore, 1758-1811. George Mann owned the City Hotel, boasting 100 beds, and served the "public entertainment" tendered by the Continental Congress "in the most elegant and profuse style" when Gen. Washington came to Annapolis to resign his commission. The Manns had seven children left orphans around 1811 (Chancery Court Records, Sept. 14, 1811).
27. Anne Arundel County Inventories, 125, f. 337, 1777.
28. See Appendix E.
29. Anne Arundel County Accounts, 72, f. 421, 1775, and Testamentary Proceedings, 47, f. 158, 1777.
30. Sally Callahan, William Buckland's granddaughter, married, March 29, 1803, Richard Harwood, the grandfather of the last private owner of the Hammond-Harwood House in Annapolis.

Index

The Abbey. *See* Ringgold house
Accotink Creek, Va., 31
Acton, Anne Arundel County, Md., 69, 161
Aikman, William, 112
Alderman Library, Univ. of Va., vii, 159
Alexandria, Va., 15, 18, 20, 28, 31, 32, 134
Allen, Rev. Bennet, 163
Allgood, William, 38
American Philosophical Society, 161
Anderson, Joseph Horatio, 70, 100
Andrews, Mr. and Mrs. Lewis W., 135
 Marietta Minnigerode, 158
Annan, Misses, 161
Annapolis, 27, 47, 48, 89, 104, 135; map, 55; descriptions of, 67 ff.; laid out, 68; architecture, 70, 71; racing day, 83 ff.; at outbreak of Revolution, 108; view, 132
Annapolis (ship), 69
Annapolis Proclamation, May 30, 1774, 105
Anne Arundel Co., Md., 72, 98, 107, 135, 160, 161, 163 ff.
Apprenticeship, 8 ff., 157
Aquia Church, Va., 14
Aquia Creek, Va., 14, 26
Architectural books, 10, 22, 27, 28, 36, 42, 91, 92, 97, 112, 149, 150
Architecture, American 18th Century, 22, 23, 92-93

Architecture, English 18th century, 9-10, 92
Ariss, John, 34, 35, 103, 159˙
Assembly Rooms (Ball Room), Annapolis 69, 100, 163
"At the Sign of the Buck," James Buckland, London bookseller, 157
Austin, Evans, 157
Ayres (Ariss), John, 34

Bailey, Samuel, 45, 147
Ball Room, Annapolis, 69, 100, 163
Ballendine, John, 31, 32
Baltimore Museum of Art, 81, 115, 135, 162
Barker, Charles A., 164
Barnes, Abraham, 19
 F. A., 159
Barr, Lockwood, 162
Barrington, Daniel, 161
Barroll, L. Wethered, 162
Beck (Negro), 147
Belleville, Richmond County, Va., 40
Belvoir, Anne Arundel Co., Md., 69, 73, 161
Belvoir, Fairfax County, Va., 21
Berkeley County, Va., 34, 159
Besant, Sir Walter, 157
Bevan, Edith Rossiter, vii
Beverley, Jane (Tayloe), Mrs. Robert, 42
 Robert, 42
 family, 42, 134, 160

CPSIA information can be obtained at www.ICGtesting.com
Printed in the USA
BVOW071049020712

294158BV00001B/31/A

9 781406 776300